Copyright © 2023 by Tiffany Dickinson

All rights reserved.

Grumblepug Press

No portion of this book may be reproduced in any form without written permission from the publisher or author, except as permitted by U.S. copyright law.

This publication is designed to provide accurate and authoritative information in regard to the subject matter covered. It is sold with the understanding that neither the author nor the publisher is engaged in rendering legal, investment, accounting, or other professional services. While the publisher and author have used their best efforts in preparing this book, they make no representations or warranties with respect to the accuracy or completeness of the contents of this book and specifically disclaim any implied warranties of merchantability or fitness for a particular purpose. No warranty may be created or extended by sales representatives or written sales materials. The advice and strategies contained herein may not be suitable for your situation. You should consult with a professional when appropriate. Neither the publisher nor the author shall be liable for any loss of profit or any other commercial damages, including but not limited to special, incidental, consequential, personal, or other damages.

Book Cover by Susansart@99designs

ISBN: 979-8-9856755-4-2

EIN: 979-8-9856755-5-9

Healing from Pet Loss

The Journey from Loving to Losing to LIving Again

Tiffany Dickinson

Grumblepug Press

This book is dedicated to the memory of Bryn,
the little pug dog who grew my heart three sizes bigger.
I will see you on the other side, sweet girl.

Contents

A Dedication	1
1. Welcome	3
2. How to Use This Book	9
3. The Stages of Grieving	12
4. Denial	16
5. Anger	22
6. Bargaining	26
7. Depression	29
8. Acceptance	37
9. Finding Meaning	41
10. My Story	45
11. Poetry	71
12. The Work of Healing	92
13. Conclusion	100

References	103
Acknowledgements	106
About the Author	108
By Tiffany Dickinson	109

A Dedication

April 28, 2022

For months on Facebook, I'd been following the saga of a sickly pug. They had bought the beloved puppy from a reputable breeder. But after he was several months old, he stopped growing and gaining weight. The conscientious owner asked the online support group for ideas and thoughts. There was a tremendous outpouring of support. People suggested everything from food allergies to the potential of poisoning.

Apparently, the vet looked at little PJ from all possible angles, and the best they could come up with was some type of autoimmune condition that affected his gut and nervous system. I don't know why, but at some point, he lost an eye related to this condition. He would bounce back, start eating his special limited diet, and then after a couple weeks the owner would be back to share that he was struggling again.

His owner seemed extremely diligent. She even drove from Tacoma to Washington State University in Pullman (about a five-hour drive) in the snow to get PJ checked out. Sadly, it was all to no avail.

Little PJ died today. He just started going downhill, and as they were on their way to the vet, the little guy was just done with the fight. I'm grateful he's in a better place. RIP beloved PJ. (That means Run in the Pasture.)

In the online forum, PJ's bereft owner asked us, "What do I do now?"

Such a profound question with so many possible answers. My heart broke that she had to walk a road so similar to mine. At that point, I knew I must write this book and share it with the world.

To answer the question, I would tell dear, kind N, "You mourn now. You mourn long and hard. You feel the pain, the anger, the disappointment, and the love and wonder you had for this being. Don't pretend it doesn't hurt, or you're not mad, or it will be okay. Because it will never be 'okay'. You'll be able to live with the facts, the pain. But that does not make it okay.

"You reminisce and wonder at the love, the hours, the money you spent. Then you smile.

"Write your shock, emptiness, your memories. You will be grateful for the reminder someday."

Seeing N's post after all these months made me desperately wish I had something to send her. A book, a record-keeping device, a plan for dealing with her grief.

So, here it is in your hands, Dear Reader. Heal well, Animal Lover.

Welcome

Walk with me, friend.
We'll prance and sniff and explore the underside
of every leaf
And one or two blades of grass
Perhaps we'll meet a friend or two along the way
But if we don't, we have each other.

You've lost a beloved pet, or someone you care about has lost a pet. Whether the loss was recent or in the distant past, you have my sympathy and love. I know the heartbreak; I've been where you are.

Perhaps you are not the animal person. What if it's a loved one who is heartbroken after a pet's passing, and you're trying to figure out how to help and support them? What if you're not even sure what the big deal is? Sometimes it hurts almost as much to see a loved one's hurt and bewilderment as it does to experience our own. You may not understand their reaction to the loss, but you want to help. A big high five to you for seeing and caring. We don't have to understand someone's pain to walk alongside them through it.

In either case, I believe this book can help you. My hope and aim is that the broken will feel whole after working through it and healing their hearts. You will know you are not alone in your sorrow and that many have suffered similarly and come out stronger and even more compassionate on the other side.

I've spent much time considering why I'm writing a book on healing from pet loss. Why me, and why now? How and why did this loss of a specific pet in my life spur me to the idea of sharing my painful experience and hopefully helping others through theirs? Who am I to write about how others can deal with the loss of a beloved pet in a healthy way?

First, I'm an animal lover – always have been, always will be. I cried about a crooked-legged colt in a children's story when I was in third grade. It was fiction, and in the story the colt grew up to be whole and strong. But it still touched my heart. I'm sure the theme of the story was that sometimes life is hard, and if we just hold on and keep trying, it will all work out okay. I'm not sure I picked up on that theme as a kid, but it's not far off from what I hope you'll find in these pages.

Life is hard – harder than most of us knew in childhood, thank God. Over time, we do learn that those who get back up and keep trying eventually get to see the vistas and bright lights in life. Don't worry, this isn't a "buck up; it will all be okay" book. I know if you're dealing with pet loss, it feels as if it will never be okay, and that's a reasonable place to be.

Second, I'm a writer. My friend, Diana Blackstone-Helt, eloquently wrote, "I think by putting into words the feelings others haven't found expression for helps readers feel they are not alone – that someone understands those feelings of guilt, anger, longing, relief, emptiness, sorrow, peace – whatever is authentic to your own experience." I love that – "putting into words the feelings others haven't found expression for" and "helps readers feel they are not alone." This is exactly what I hope sharing this book and my story with you will do.

We've all experienced losses – some small, some great, and we all have some big feelings around these losses. However, not everyone can put words to those feelings, especially when we are in the pain's epicenter. So, I'm sharing *my* words with you. I'll give you some ideas for those who would like to put some feelings down on paper – to remember their beloved, or simply to get the thoughts out of their head.

The other half of the statement, "to help readers feel they are not alone", is huge. Until we've experienced a significant loss, we cannot truly understand what others have lived. If you don't have people close to you who understand your bond with your pet, or who don't at least respect it if they can't understand it, then you can feel doubly alone. But you are not alone in your love or in your grief. Sometimes it's an older animal, and their passing is not unexpected. It may even be a relief, but that does not diminish the pain, loss, and emptiness that pet leaves in our homes and lives.

Too many of us experience what's termed "traumatic pet loss." This happens when a pet dies unexpectedly by illness or accident, is lost and never found, or is abandoned against the owner's will, such as what may happen in cases of natural disasters like floods, hurricanes, and fires. Animals (just like people) often panic and head for the hills when they feel threatened.

Research findings show that pet owners who've lost their pets or have been forced to abandon them because of a natural disaster experience higher levels of traumatic stress than those who experience the disaster without pets. Feelings of guilt may compound the impact as well. If you are in such a situation, know that you're not alone in your heartbreak and grief.

News flash: Our pets are important to us. The 2017-18 American Veterinary Medical Association (AVMA) reported that 80% of pet owners consider the animals in their homes family members. Of course, this doesn't surprise you or me. Whether you call your beloved animal your fur baby, companion, pet, family member, child, or whatever, you love them and sacrifice for them. For most pet owners, taking good care of their pets is a financial commitment. Add in time, energy, picking up after, walking, cleaning, vet trips, arranging sitters – human family members sometimes feel easier! Non-animal people don't understand, and we must forgive them. I'm also sorry for them, but that's for another day. The point is, this book is for animal lovers – or someone trying to understand an animal lover. So, welcome aboard the furry train!

I hope you don't think your grief is selfish or means that you lack faith. Of course, we grieve for our own losses. We mourn the companionship, the intimacy, the hopes, dreams, and plans that are now dissolved into thin air. We are also broken-hearted for the lost future of the other. Our Bryn never got a chance to go to the beach or run around the yard with our granddaughter or meet our grandson. A world of people will never see her spunk, love, and personality. Our other pets are missing out as well. So, I don't mourn only for myself. I regret a world without Bryn. Hurting is not selfish; it is evidence of love.

We love our animals, and part of loving anyone is to hurt when they're gone. Why write (or read) about pet loss when it's simply an experience to "get through?" You and I know there are healthy, safe ways, as well as unhealthy, destructive ways, to get through difficult times. Wallowing and soaking ourselves in alcohol or online shopping are destructive, unhealthy ways. Remembering our beloved through written words, shared stories, and comforting thoughts are healthy, uplifting ways of coping. There are other positive ways to grieve, remember, and honor, and I hope you'll find your own unique expressions and rituals as you read this book and grow through your grieving experience.

Writing about grief matters to me because I wanted to process the loss of my 10-month-old puppy, Bryn, against the backdrop of other losses in my life. She died due to a genetic neurological disease called Pug Dog Encephalitis (PDE). I also want to help others who've suffered similarly, to validate their feelings and experiences and help them work through them. Through this book and other resources, I hope you'll discover your own words to define your experience and use them to grow, flourish, and live again.

Losing a puppy years before her prime – many years before her time should have been up – spurred me to create this book. I had lost pets before, but most had lived beautiful, long lives, and their passings were not unexpected or unreasonable. I have grieved for them all in varying degrees. Some of these losses I've felt deeper than others, depending on how the pet died, how old they were, and what other things were happening in our lives. Sometimes, when you're dealing with family stressors, impending moves, and job changes, an elderly pet passing on releases you from one more responsibility. But often it's not that simple, and we react much more strongly. However our pets left us, I loved them all and miss them still. We talk and reminisce about them all – just like family. Don't you?

However, the unexpected sudden decline and subsequent death of the puppy was a blow unlike any I'd experienced. Since childhood, I had dreamed of having this dog breed (pug). My husband made the dream come true for me after his retiring from the military, and we had become empty-nesters. He found a fantastic professional breeder, and we were off!

Bryn lived with us from age eight weeks to 10 months, and then she was gone. It felt like the cruelest, most shocking thing I had experienced in 50 years of life.

So, after laying my broken heart on page after page, I grew through the experience. Then, I began to hear other animal lovers who had lost pets – really *hear* them. I heard their hearts, not only their words. Realizing it was my heart also, I felt with much soul searching and checking in with people I respect, that I might help somehow.

So, if you are grieving the loss of a pet for any reason, or you care about someone in that situation, this book is for you. My prayer is that you will find camaraderie and comfort in these pages. When the time is right, I hope your heart (scarred but stronger) will be ready to love another worthy creature. For they are all worthy.

How to Use This Book

broken hearts can heal
but know the beautiful scar
will always remain

If you've loved an animal that loved you back, then this book has something for you. Loving an animal differs from loving a person. We expect things from people – even young children – if we're honest. We expect them to love us back, show a semblance of respect, some kind of reward at the end of the road of raising them – like them not ending up on America's Most Wanted. That's not asking for much!

With animals, we just ask that they be there, right? Often, we ask them to be companions, helpers, and comfort animals, but we don't expect them to support us in our old age or even now! Often all we really want or need is for them to lie beside us while we watch TV or exercise or cry or rant about fill-in-the-blank. "Whatever those jerks out in the world think of me, you still like me, right? I'll feed you, clean up your space, take you outside, and rub your belly. I'll spend ridiculous amounts of money on vets, toys, special beds, special food bowls, and more. Just be with me and please don't die." Then they do. Die, I mean. Because that's what all living things do eventually, either too early, right on time, or too late. Whenever it is, we all die eventually. And with a beloved animal, it's always too early – even when they've lived for 20 years.

Why do we love them so much, so deeply? They love us. They don't judge or criticize. Although they may try to boss us around, they would kill or die for us. The animals soak up our love and time and money, and we (mostly) give it happily. Because, what's the alternative? Allow this creature to leave our lives? Hope someone else cares as much as we do? Heaven forbid.

So please read on, based on where you are on the healing continuum. If your pain is new and raw, then reading the sections on the stages of grieving can help you recognize where you are and where your feelings are coming from. My story leading to the creation of this book is in the second part. If you love poetry and would like some inspiration in using the written word to honor the memory of your pet, flip back to the Poetry section. Jump around. There is no one right way to use this book.

If you have just lost your pet and are simply trying to make it through the day, starting with the Stages of Grieving section to better understand what you are going through will probably be most helpful.

The last section of the book, The Work of Healing, contains a list of 30 activities to help you on your healing path and to memorialize your pet. Listed at the end of the book are the references I used, as well as some online resources.

Note: Although I have a master's degree in nursing and in the past have worked with terminally ill patients and their families, I am not, nor have I ever been, a grief or mental health care clinician. Also, I am not currently certified to provide medical or mental health diagnoses or clinical or pharmaceutical prescriptions. Therefore, nothing mentioned in this book is meant to be prescriptive or to take the place of the care and expertise of a licensed healthcare professional.

Now, are you ready to embark on your healing journey? Blessings to you. Let's begin!

The Stages of Grieving

the sorrowing heart
is an expert on the taste
of clouds and sunshine

Psychiatrist Elizabeth Kubler-Ross published her findings related to the five stages of grieving in her 1969 book *On Death and Dying*. Kubler-Ross had worked for years with terminally ill patients. Over time, she conceptualized a framework of the grief experience related to dying that has stood the test of time. During my years at university studying to be a nurse, I learned about the concepts and framework. Not all grief experts or grief sufferers support Kubler-Ross's theory. However, it is a clear framework clinicians have used for many years, and countless individuals have found it helpful.

The stages of grief are Denial, Anger, Bargaining, Depression, and Acceptance. In his book, *Finding Meaning*, David Kessler, Kubler-Ross's protégé and co-author, added a sixth stage. Through several decades of working with grieving individuals and experiencing his own traumatic grief, Kessler discovered that many grieving people at some point come to a place of finding meaning related to the loss. I've included the sixth stage, Finding Meaning, in our discussion as well.

We don't always go through these stages in the same order, nor does every person experience all of them, but this is the most common sequence. Also, we don't always move sequentially through the stages. A grieving person may cycle through stages, coming back to one or more, multiple times. For example, in the midst of your sadness, you may experience anger at someone else related to the loss of your pet. Grief takes time to be laid down, and it is likely to raise its head frequently, reminding you it's still there.

It all falls within the realm of normal. Kubler-Ross identified these stages for most persons experiencing grief and loss. She also acknowledged what I've mentioned: each person may experience it differently and in a different sequence.

While we're not going to officially diagnose your reaction to loss, I'm sharing these five stages because I believe they're important for you to know. The more you understand your grief responses, the better equipped you will be to ride the tumultuous waves of emotions.

Realizing you're not the only person who's experienced anger or tried to bargain their way out of a painful situation can be comforting. It can help you feel you are not so alone. If the loss leaves you feeling utterly abandoned, you can be reassured that you have not lost your mind or "gone off the deep end".

Will knowing these stages relieve the pain? Probably not. Will knowing the stages make them go by quicker? Possibly, but it's not likely. I think the major benefit of knowing the basics of the grief stages is so we can use it as a sort of temperature gauge. If you can step back far enough, you may be able to tell "where you're at" on your grief journey.

For example, if you start playing the blame game or throwing angry fire darts, you may be able to decipher your feelings and say, "Maybe this is bargaining. When I say, 'If only the vet had done…,' I realize I'm blaming, and that's a normal part of the denial phase." This awareness can remind us that spewing on social media or threatening to sue everyone involved is usually not the healthiest choice. Hopefully, with time, we can let the feelings pass on.

Sadly, sometimes negligence or avoidable fault is involved. In that case, seeking legal or civil justice may help your healing process. I am not suggesting you jump into the court system while you're grieving heavily. Nothing will bring our beloved back to us. However, the consequences for a negligent or guilty person or persons may help to ensure that another pet and pet lover won't have to suffer the way you have. This book offers no legal advice, but if you feel that malpractice or abuse has occurred, and you have the emotional fortitude to pursue it, I encourage you to seek sound legal counsel.

Although these stages were first identified in people who were dying, they are just as valid in the loss of an animal or experiencing another traumatic event, such as a loss of limb or physical ability, or home devastation. Loss is loss, and if you lose something you care about, whether it's a person, pet, identity, or ability, you will grieve.

You might ask, "Will I ever feel whole again?" That's a good question. During awful pain, it overruns everything. It feels as if the pain is our entire existence, and we will never be free of it. You *will* feel normal again. However, it will be a new normal.

I look at photos of myself before Bryn died, and I feel as I'm looking at a different person. That ecstasy of holding my dream puppy makes me seem almost innocent in the photos – not knowing what I would endure down the road. Even now, we don't know what we will endure in the future. I count that as a blessing of not being omniscient. You *will* feel whole again

— a new whole. A new part or facet has been added, but you will have new strength and wisdom.

Allow yourself to be angry, sad, or blaming. Give grief the time it needs. Virtually every human goes through loss and most have come through it stronger, and often more empathetic than before. Allow yourself love and grace in the same way you would another grieving person, or even a pet that is suffering.

Knowledge is power. Knowing the stages of grieving and that you are likely to go through each one can help you be gentle with yourself and not wonder why you are "taking so long to get over it". Pain is pain. Can you make your sprained ankle feel better by telling it not to hurt? Write to me if you can! Our hearts and feelings are the same. We can't talk ourselves out of sadness. We can cover it up, pretend it isn't there, shunt our energy somewhere else, but it will come out eventually, and usually at an inconvenient time. So, take time for grief. Give it space and eventually the grief that seems to have enveloped you will feel smaller as you grow around it.

Anything you feel is normal. Recently, I was on an airplane flight with a group of writers, and one of them mentioned feeling weird when telling people about her writing. A fellow writer said, "Anything you feel is normal." That phrase struck me as something true we all can embrace. Let's not pathologize our feelings soon after a loss. Let's feel them, sit with them, and see what, if anything, we should do. Anything you feel after losing your pet is normal. Remember that. Remember, also every person is not lucky enough to have the love we've received.

Denial

I look at your puppy pictures.
But that is not you. Unfinished, infantile.
What I miss is the full-grown heft, the smell of you. Your understanding.
How can you be gone? It is incomprehensible to me that something
so alive, bursting with life, is no more.
A dead weight of flesh and fur reduced to ashes in a box.
No, it can't be.
Too clunky to be a dragonfly,
You are a butterfly in flight.

The first stage of grief is denial. We can experience denial before, during, or after the passing of our pet. It may be fleeting, such as the thought, "No, this can't happen." Or it can go on for a while. If you're reading this, you've most likely passed through denial and are in a different phase, but it's still important to be aware of the signs.

During the denial phase, we may say things like, "This can't be happening," or "The veterinarian is wrong," or "She just has to get better."

Denial can even happen after the pet passes. In some extreme cases, the pet owner may choose to believe someone stole the pet, or the vet didn't really euthanize them but sold them for some nefarious reason. These types of experiences support the argument for being present during euthanasia if possible. Animal advocates also recommend the owner be present as it can calm the pet, and we can be assured that their last thoughts were not, "Where are they? Why did they leave me?"

It's a very personal decision and can be a tough call. I've never been present for the euthanizing of a pet. I was afraid that I would relive that moment on loop forever. However, after what I've learned, I won't shy away from being there for those last moments in the future. Only you can decide what is best for you. In the end, know that your beloved pet is filled with the love you've given them. They don't blame you for being human. That's why they love you.

I didn't even want to see Bryn's body after she died "naturally", but my husband gently prodded me to go see her, and it was absolutely the right thing to do. I would regret it if I hadn't.

In my past, I was an oncology nurse and worked with patients who were terminally ill for various other medical reasons. I've seen death's approach and its finality. But watching the life ebb from my beloved pet to nothing just wasn't what I had strength for at the time. You'll get no judgement from me.

However, there are benefits of being with your pet as they are gently ushered into the next life. You can know that they weren't wondering where you were. You can be reassured of exactly how carefully and gently the vet care staff handled your loved one. Singing to them, telling them how good they are, and how much you love them can be healing for you. It can be beautiful and even healing for many pet owners. The pet-lover can see what actually happened, that no one dropped their beloved friend, put them in a dumpster, or sold them for research. (By the way, that is not something most people need to concern themselves with, but sometimes during a state of extreme grief, we can get weird ideas.) Being with your pet as it passes on helps with closure, but no one should press the pet-lover to watch, especially if they are a child. That should go without saying. Each person involved should receive gentle encouragement and support for what they can handle.

You may know exactly what you're going to do when the time comes. Or it may take you by surprise. Sadly for my family, we've had only one or two pet deaths for which we could plan. The others have been sudden and almost emergent. It's tough to make good decisions when that happens. We all just do the best we can at the time.

As a parent and grandparent, I recommend not having children present during euthanasia. Allowing them to say their goodbyes to the living animal is probably best. I'm sure different veterinary offices have different policies regarding this. There are possible exceptions. If the child insists, after having everything explained, or the procedure will take place at home with plenty of support, it may work fine. You know your child and their ability to handle things. Death is a part of life and is best not treated as a scary anomaly.

No one of any age should be required to watch euthanasia or look at the lifeless body if they don't care to. While I'm on my soapbox, let's be truthful as well. The animal didn't go to a "farm" and didn't "get adopted by a nice family". Also, saying a pet was "put to sleep" or "went to sleep" can be very scary for a child. They may never want to sleep after that, or they may wonder when the pet will wake up and come back. We expect honesty from others; trust is a two-way street. Life hurts sometimes, and one big responsibility of parents and grandparents is to comfort the children during loss and pain, even amidst our own struggles.

The grief experience doesn't only occur during or after a hard event. Many of us experience anticipatory grieving. As we watch our pet aging or live with the awareness that they have a serious medical diagnosis with a ticking clock, we know their departure isn't far away. We can react to this in several ways, and denial can play a big part. Taking on excessively high financial costs and putting our pets through extreme treatments that will probably be ineffective are demonstrations of denial. Treating the pet the same way, such as expecting them to take walks or eat the same food they always have, may be forms of denial as well.

Of course, we could be angry too. That can lead to bargaining, in which we may say, "If I pay all this money or do all these treatments, that will do the trick. They can't help but get better."

One danger of denial is that we can't heal or move forward in this state. Denial could take the form of not being able to admit that an animal is critically ill and needs either treatment or a merciful passing. Denial may cause us to leave things as they are. If we never clean up the space left by the ill animal or wash their things, that's a sign of denial. Refusing to gift unneeded and impersonal items to others who could use them can also be a sign of denial.

I am absolutely not suggesting that you clear everything out the hour, or even the day or week, you return from the vet. I would even caution against washing or tossing anything (unless it's soiled with blood or body fluids that are causing your home to be unclean or unsafe) right away. One of my regrets after Bryn passed was that I washed all her stuff immediately – bed, toys, blanket. It just seemed like the thing to do. Soon afterward, I realized I had nothing that smelled like her. Although I journaled about sharing the scented blanket with the cat before tossing it into the wash, it didn't occur to me to stop and hold on to it.

I try to be a diligent pet mom, and I wash all our dogs' blankets, bedding, and toys regularly. So, it seemed natural to do so. But then nothing, and I mean *nothing*, smelled like her anymore. I missed her little sweaty head smell. Every dog has a unique smell (even if you bathe them regularly, it comes back within a couple of days). Just like humans, I guess. Our sense of smell is practically nonexistent compared to a dog's (which I'm sure is a blessing sometimes). I gently suggest keeping at least a couple of things out of the wash for a while, such as your pet's favorite toy or their blanket if it's not too soiled. This can be very comforting – for you and for other animals in the home. Regardless of how the other pets act, they know one is missing.

If you have anything of the lost pet's with their scent still on it, it's okay for the surviving pets to sniff them. Of course, they remember the lost animal. Although we cannot explain to them in human language what's happened, the scent may be comforting to them. If it's workable, allowing the other pets to view and sniff the deceased animal may be beneficial for them. They can discern a living thing from one not living, and it can give them closure. This doesn't mean they won't miss the other animal and even grieve, but they won't be wondering why their companion just "disappeared" or where they went. They instinctively know death.

As a survival mechanism, denial is one of nature's ways of allowing us to continue functioning without a total system breakdown. People get through huge stressors of illness, loss, or national tragedy while enveloped in a light cloak of denial. This is okay. God help the person who tries to confront the freshly grieving with reality. Why anyone would do that, I wonder.

Trying to move past denial is only a necessary goal if your activities of daily life are being compromised. As long as you're eating enough, bathing, sleeping, caring for your other pets and children or whomever is in your realm of responsibility, you're okay to stay "under the cloak" of denial for a while. If other pets or family members or your own health needs are being neglected, get some help. Otherwise, just give your grief and denial space. Reality (likely carrying a nice baggage set of anger with it) will set in soon enough.

When Bryn first displayed atypical signs and symptoms (walking in small circles, decreased eating, inactivity), the vet and I worked up all kinds of angles. "Maybe she's in pain." "Maybe she has allergies." It did not occur to me that this perfect dog could have a hereditary condition that would kill her. Even when the seizures started two days before she died, although I was extremely upset, I thought, "Oh, a neurologist will figure this out. Maybe she has epilepsy. We have pet health insurance for her."

The two things I remember the emergency vet saying the night before Bryn died are, "It's good you have pet insurance; this is what it's for." And "Look up pugs with seizures online when you get home." I should have known what was coming as we left, since Bryn hardly responded to us, just lying quietly in the cage. But denial and hope are powerful things.

When we got home that night after leaving Bryn at the emergency vet with the seizure bell collar on, my husband Paul looked it up. "You should look at this."

Sitting on the bed, hugging my legs, I said, "No, I don't want to." That's what denial is. People are trying to tell you what's happening, or you see it with your own eyes, and you refuse to listen or to believe it. Again, it's an emotional survival mechanism.

You may move quickly through the denial stage, or it may linger. Be gentle with yourself. It won't last forever, and the feelings that follow are likely to be as sharp as a fillet knife.

Anger

Today, I feel like one of those zombie dolls I hate,
with X's for eyes.
Sewed up, but not real. Not whole. Not really alive,
but pretending to be, with a fake creepy smile on my face.

At some point, reality kicks in, and the cold, hard truth of our hurt is sitting in the middle of the room like the proverbial elephant. As soon as we recognize it for what it is, the next stage of grief arrives from the wings. Its name is Anger.

Anger. What else is there to say? Everything we tried to stop the inevitable or deny the truth of what's happened hasn't brought back our pet or changed the facts. They're gone, and they're not coming back to where we are. We may be furious that our beloved was taken from us, or angry that they had to suffer. We may blame the vet for not catching it sooner. Or we rail that the treatment was too expensive and that could have saved them. We may think we want to sue the breeder for providing us with a "defective" animal.

Not everyone experiences anger, but many of us do. We can be disgusted with ourselves for caring so much. Of course, you and I love animals, but we may say, "Why should I feel so strongly about this when other people are suffering greater losses? There are people who've lost *people*, for God's sake! What am I whining about?" These are valid questions, and they may help us put our feelings into perspective at some point. You know as well as I do our animals are people to us and many of us trust and rely on our animals more than we've ever been able to trust or rely on a human. If you're feeling chagrined at your own potent feelings, please be gentle with yourself. Your feelings are valid. This creature was and is important. You have every right to feel disappointed and bereft by their passing.

Our anger may rekindle when we think our pet's death could have been avoided. Bitter feelings toward our family, friends, neighbors, or coworkers can seep in if they don't seem to care as much as we think they should. They certainly don't seem to understand what we're going through. Morosely, we think the sun shouldn't shine. How dare it? Worse yet, how dare other people be joyful in their own lives?

If we're lucky, we have an animal friends support group – fellow pet lovers that we regularly commune with. I belong to two online pug groups where I can share questions, concerns, silly stories, and adorable pictures. On a down day, I can look at pictures and videos of newborn puppies within the pug-loving families and feel some of the joy of cuddly new life. When something hard happens related to my pets, I know exactly where I can go to get empathetic support and truly heartfelt virtual hugs. I encourage you to find the same. I list several online resources near the end of this book.

Anger is a natural and normal part of the grieving process. We might be vexed with God. After all, doesn't He love you and your pet? I believe He does. God also has given us the ability to feel and to have free will. Emotions and feelings are an integral and expected part of the human experience.

They are not wrong and can be expressed at the appropriate times and places.

If you keep cycling through anger at your partner because they talked you out of taking your pet to the vet that one last time, you have a right to that anger – for a while. However, you must lay it to rest at some point. Even if your partner admits they should have encouraged the vet visit, you may still be angry. Remember that had you followed a different course, you may have ended up in the same place.

It's not uncommon for a person to turn their anger toward themself – for not being more assertive and insisting on the vet visit, in the previous example. These are all natural responses. Most of us make choices every single day we'd have done differently if we'd known the outcome in advance. Nothing can be done. We are not seers. We do the best we can at the time. Decisions must lie as they are. We all constantly live with the consequences of our decisions – from years past to five minutes ago. That is what makes up a life.

Mishandled anger or lingering bitterness can be destructive. Left unchecked, it will damage our relationships with others, especially when we perceive blame or guilt. Anger turned inward may lead to self-destructive behaviors, such as overeating, over-drinking, and indulging in other unhealthy behaviors. Lingering resentment will pave the way for us to withdraw from others or cut people from our lives, even when it's not warranted.

Throughout my grieving process after losing Bryn, I denied feeling angry. If asked, I would have said, "I have no anger, just sadness." And I would have meant it. However, looking back, I see that I definitely carried resentment with me. A couple of months after Bryn died, during my journaling, I composed a document entitled "Sins of the Vet". In it, I listed all the things I felt the regular vet office and staff (not emergency vet) had done wrong in the weeks prior to Bryn's death and the weeks following.

Some were legitimate complaints (not legal or moral issues, but things the vet and office could have handled better). Others were just me being hurt and looking for someone to blame. I did nothing with the document until writing this. I doubt I would ever confront the office with a list of complaints because they never had the intention to harm.

Amazingly to me, I never felt anger toward the breeder who unknowingly bred two dogs (from award-winning AKC lines) carrying the gene that killed Bryn. Since then, that breeding community has carefully tested every dog they plan to breed. It's not an easy or inexpensive test, but it's the right thing to do. Ideally, pug breeders would breed the genetic defect out of existence. This is one of many reasons backyard breeders and puppy mills (which are not the same thing but carry some of the same risks) are such a scourge on the healthy purebred population and often disastrous for the dogs and new owners.

Through the testing efforts of our breeder and her network, perhaps our experience with Bryn has saved others from heartache. I've always felt as if the professional breeders were doing the best they could, and they cared about the dogs. I still believe that.

Anger needs room to burn itself out. Whether we write it out in a journal, day after day, or we talk it out with a friend, or we punch it out in a pillow, it needs a safe place for expression. You can write an accusing letter to whomever you want, then destroy it. You can paint a blank canvas black, then stomp on it. Chop wood until your back hurts (don't throw your back out, and keep far from anyone else while you're holding the axe). Feel it. Let it out. Express it. You will not always be mad. If your anger is affecting your daily life, then speak with a mental health professional who can help you work through your feelings. Typically, anger will wear itself out after a while. We often eventually get to where we think we can outrun or con this grief out of getting the better of us. That's when we move into the bargaining phase.

Bargaining

such a little thing
such a little thing to ask
stay with me friend, stay

During the bargaining stage, the reality of our situation sinks in. Sure there's still some way to derail this train, we may say to God or the universe, "If you get her through this, I promise to do such-and-such." Or "If we can have just one more year, I'll never do (fill in the blank) again."

If our pet has already passed, during bargaining we may say things such as, "If only I had…" or "Why didn't they…" Guilt, shame, or blaming is not uncommon during this phase. We may experience fear or anxiety that we may lose another pet or loved one or that some other tragedy will befall us or our family.

Regardless of fault, we often feel guilt related to the death of a loved one. Perhaps we think we were negligent. We may entertain thoughts such as, "If I had gotten him to the vet sooner…" or "If I had noticed his symptoms sooner…" or "If I'd been more attentive…". Even if we know there was absolutely nothing we could do to stop the inevitable, we can wonder, "Did I love her enough? Was I patient enough? Did I spend enough time with him?" These thoughts are normal. If we have any kind of life aside from our pets, such as family, work, or volunteer commitments, we're going to spend time away from them. We live our lives, of which our pet is a significant part, but not the only part. Remember, one reason you're hurting so much is that you *did* love enough, and that you *were* paying attention and you're missing the object of your attention.

If you're feeling guilty for something that you should have and could have impacted, then now is the time to address it. Write or share your feelings with someone you trust. Then see if and how you can make amends. Perhaps there's a hole in the fence that needs mending. Resolve to fix it now. Perhaps the pet was left with a distracted person. Start investigating reliable pet sitters for the future. Thoughtfully prepare for your next love.

We are human, therefore we are not perfect. We will make mistakes and have blind spots. It isn't humanly possible (if we are to stay sane) to prepare for every eventuality. Try to set things up so this situation won't cause future pain. When making decisions, I often ask myself, "What will your future self thank you for?"

You loved this creature, you provided for them, and they know you loved them. What more, besides food, shelter, a safe space to rest and play, and snuggles, can an animal hope for? To be loved unconditionally by a human, as they loved unconditionally, is their highest calling. Your pet met its highest calling on this earth by loving you. Honor that.

We may feel guilty toward our surviving pets. Perhaps we expected another one would leave us first, rather than the one that did. Or we may be concerned that the surviving pet didn't get enough attention during the lost pet's illness or after death. This is when we must remind ourselves of our pets' forgiving natures. Animals are models of forgiveness; something we could strive to emulate. Our pets will not remember our absentmindedness, and they can't read our thoughts. Just love them the best you can now.

During your time of grief, try to avoid overindulging the surviving pets. You may give them a few extra treats or let them snuggle with you on the couch when that wasn't allowed before, but keep their health in mind, and don't establish a habit with them you don't intend to continue. That will only increase their confusion and everybody's stress farther down the road.

In the bargaining phase, we think of all the things we'll do, say, or think if only things can go back to the way they were before. We may construct deals, trying to placate whatever powers-that-be that put us in this situation. It's painful, it's hard, and it doesn't work. Bargaining does not cure cancer, grow limbs back, or raise a loved one from the dead, no matter what the witch doctor says. Most of us figure this out pretty quickly and move on to the most difficult and saddest of the stages, which is depression.

Depression

The grieving silently weep themselves to sleep.
If you have done so, you are my brother.

When depression or sadness comes, the truth has hit us squarely in the chest. It's no longer the elephant in the room, but the skin on our bones. The pain may even feel as if it's *inside* our bones. Reality is upon us, and it sucks. This is the bone-crushing weariness, the waking up crying, the stomach upset of grief.

This is the stage most people mean when they say "grief". It's split our broken heart open, and we don't even care to mop up the contents and try to shove them back in. We have lost something precious and irreplaceable. Just as people are unique and no person can replace another, animals are also unique and cannot simply be replaced.

Near my lowest point, I remember asking, "How much saltwater can one adult human produce? How many nights can I cry before I'm deemed mentally ill?" There was no answer to these rhetorical questions. I just had to take it one day at a time. It feels like it's always worst at night. You can't call anyone; you don't want to text anyone. It's just you and your pain.

Depression will probably stay with you longer than any stage other than acceptance. We can grieve well, but trying to rush through and "get over it" doesn't work.

American culture is uncomfortable with grief. The grieving are admonished with phrases such as, "They are no longer in pain," "Other people have it so much worse", or "You should count your blessings." Most people who say these things are well-meaning, and the statements are true. However, they are useless and dishonoring platitudes that encourage the mourning to stuff their feelings and pretend they haven't suffered a tremendous loss.

"It's better to have loved and lost than never to have loved at all." I've never regretted what loss has taught me. I would much rather have my heart broken than never know love. But this is something for us to tell ourselves after we've healed, not when we're just trying to make it through the day.

During my pain, I wrote, "I wouldn't wish this on my worst enemy." I still feel that way. I might wish a million fire ants to swarm their bed, but I wouldn't wish the pain of the loss of a beloved pet to them.

For many of us, our animal companion is our comfort. They spend the most time with us, never judging or complaining. They will sit with us, sleep with us, walk with us – even when we were a grouchy bear this morning, or we didn't take them walking yesterday. Loved animals don't hold grudges or demand reciprocity. Sometimes, our jobs or families or life are hard to deal with, and the pet's presence in our world keeps us sane. Then they're gone. What do you do when your comforter is not there to comfort you?

Consider the idea that grief equals loving. When we grieve the passing of someone, it is a sign of the esteem with which we beheld them. It is not a sign of maladjustment or imbalance or unhealthy dependence. Grieving the loss of someone is a sign that you love them deeply.

Depression can show up in many ways. The expected reactions of crying, loss of appetite, or moroseness will probably be part of your experience. You may also notice decreased joy or appreciation for things that previously brought you pleasure. You might be more tired and desire to sleep more than usual or want to sleep all the time. Wanting to withdraw from people or feeling unable to go places and be with others who were part of your life with your pet may be part of your experience.

It may help you feel better to volunteer at a shelter or veterinarian's office. But that may not come until later. If you've already been volunteering when your pet passes, only you can decide if you need a break from that role or if being around the other animals comforts you. There is no wrong answer.

Remember that the sadness is real, it's not indulgent, and the more we allow ourselves to live the experience, the easier the transition to healing will be. Grieving deeply and honestly is not wallowing. We will heal best if we feel the pain and work through it, acknowledging our loss experience.

If you experience joy, don't hold yourself back. However, if you feel like a certain person or activity is more than you can handle or deal with now, you have every right to protect yourself. Other people, even those who love us, don't always know what we need. Even though they can help sometimes, we're usually the best person to decide what's right for us.

Sometimes, sadness can easily swing back into anger. Anger can be a mask for sadness and vice versa. You don't have to decipher the symptoms. Just try to go with them, hurting no one in anger.

The phrase "Grief is feral" resonates with me. My dictionary provides such synonyms for feral as "wild", "ferocious", and "brutal". I would add "unpredictable". Grief has a mind of its own. We cannot control it.

Our cat Lola is part feral, meaning the animal shelter workers found a box of kittens on their front porch one morning. She has never been fully domesticated. Living virtually her entire life in a comfortable, safe home with all the cat amenities, kept strictly indoors for her own safety, she is still skittish, hates strangers, and will bite and claw without warning. She can be loving, but watch out! That's what feral is. Unpredictable, uncontrollable.

During this time, you may experience physical symptoms that are not typical for you. If they last longer than a few days, note when the changes began and how long they last. These symptoms can be because of the emotions around loss, but sometimes people really have a physical ailment that needs medical attention. They may chalk the symptoms up to grief, stress, or depression. Then later, they find themselves dealing with something that could have been helped with appropriate medical intervention. So, get checked out. Take care of yourself. Even if you think this exhaustion and muscle ache is "all in your head", perhaps your primary healthcare provider can do a few tests to rule out anything alarming.

My personal (not professional) opinion is to avoid taking anti-depressant medication right away. Unless you have an actual clinical diagnosis of depression or another mental health condition that warrants it or you are in danger of harming yourself, give it time. I am not currently a licensed clinician and am not giving medical advice. However, many of us have seen people given a pill prescription when what they really needed was some support, counseling, and time.

Antidepressant medications have their place, and a healthy grief response may or may not be that place. You could try a pharmaceutical course of action, see how you feel in three months (or however long you and your clinician agree upon), then revisit the situation. Then you could decide if it's time to stop the medication, add a medication, or leave things as is. Mental health drugs are not benign. They have potential side effects that aren't pleasant. So please consider all options that align with your values. It's your body, your healing, your life.

Soon after Bryn died, someone said to me, "Dealing with grief is like living in a rock tumbler." Doesn't that conjure up an image? We don't know if we're coming or going, or when or where it's going to hit next. It's exhausting.

During the grieving process, we may feel as if death is everywhere. It is ever-present, constant, and guaranteed. Weeks after Bryn's death, I realized that I more easily noticed sadness in others and death nearby. Those things were no longer "out there" in the world, reported in the horrifying news, but close to home. I felt others' pain more than I ever had – the heartbreak of the mental decline of a loved one, lost pets, damaged relationships. It was as if losing Bryn had turned my emotional pain receptors on high so that I felt everything. I absorbed the pain like a chameleon takes on other colors or a butterfly whose feet taste the surface they walk on. When I stepped onto the tear-filled ground, it welled up in me.

Organizations can be just as guilty as thoughtless people. With so much automation and internet traffic and marketing, it's easy for some information to get lost in the shuffle. Things happen such as receiving a "Happy Birthday" message for your deceased pet months later from a vet or pet supply store. At best, we may feel grateful and savor the bittersweetness of the remembrance. On the other hand, it may jar us out of a quiet day where we thought we had it under control. Then, just like that, we're back in grief, missing our pet on their birthday and cursing the innocent sender. It sure makes for a quick unsubscribe, warranted or not.

Here are some things you might say to a grieving person even when you're uncomfortable or don't understand their pain: "You are not alone." "I'm listening." "I'm here with you." "I hear you." Our physical actions and attitudes can show most of these sentiments and often don't need to be stated. As they say, "Just do it." It's not possible for us to understand everything anyone has gone through. But we can say, "I know you're hurting, and I'm here for you."

Of course, since you're reading this book, I'm going to assume you'd never say something such as, "It's only a dog/cat/bird." Or "They wouldn't want you to be sad." Or "It was just an animal. Many people have lost more than that." We're all here (you and me) because we care about people who love animals, and we want them to heal well, not hide their pain due to shame or misunderstanding.

If you've lost a pet, find a supportive person. They can be another pet lover or a professional if that's a better choice for you. The world is full of pet lovers. Contact your vet office if you feel comfortable doing so. A good vet will have resources to share with you to help support you through the grief experience. There's a vast variety in what veterinarian offices offer and how helpful they are. So, if your vet's office is limited in that area, call around for referrals and resources if you feel comfortable.

This time of depression can make us very vulnerable. I don't mean just vulnerable in our feelings or sensitivity, but vulnerable to others who may not have our best interests at heart. We've heard about people who got married too soon after a spouse passed away, and it didn't go well. Or about grieving people who got scammed by so-called "ambulance chasers" or "do-gooders" who were anything but.

When I came out of the fog of depression, I realized that in the previous couple of months, my Facebook friend number had doubled. After I posted about Bryn's death and my broken heart, the outpouring of love was more of a response than I'd ever had before on social media. This shows that many people empathize with the loss of a beloved pet. It's common ground that scores of people share. Later, I realized I had somehow responded to the "love" from people I didn't know because of the hole in my heart. I subconsciously wanted to gather more of it to me. So, anyone and everyone who sent me a friend request got accepted; I wasn't paying attention at all.

So far, nothing harmful has come from my growing Facebook friend list. But occasionally when I get a comment on my personal page, I'll say, "How do I know this person?" I usually chalk it up to that period after Bryn passed. When I came out of the fog, I realized how vulnerable a person could be in this situation. If I lived alone or didn't have good support after the loss, someone with nefarious intentions could have easily wormed their way into my life. Beware, Dear Reader. Guard your heart. I don't want you to wake up from your grief fog in a new terrible situation you must dig out from.

Not long after Bryn's death, I said, "I don't want to live in a world where there's no Bryn." It wasn't that I had lost my will to live, but it felt as if all the color had drained right out of the world. I knew I'd continue living, but all I saw were dull grays, blacks, whites, though it was mid-summer. I likened it to an old black-and-white TV, not sharp black and white, like an Ansel Adams picture.

When we have these kinds of feelings and thoughts, we must be careful. I felt I could easily pass into the next life with no hesitation, just to be with her. Fortunately, I was nowhere near taking steps, and I was aware enough to know that if I had suicidal thoughts, I would tell someone. There were days I thought that if I just went to sleep and didn't wake up, that would have been okay, because I would see Bryn. If these types of thoughts are persistent for you, talk to someone helpful — a wise person (or the crisis line itself) who can help you sort out your feelings and make sure you're safe.

You may feel as if slipping from this earthly plane would be so much more comfortable than what you're feeling now. No more pain – and you would be with your sweetie. Don't be shocked to feel that way. No emotionally healthy person *wants* to be in pain. Give it time. One day at a time, one step after the other. Do the things that need doing. Help the people and animals who need you. Then one day you'll find you went an hour or half a day without feeling sad or hopeless. You were busy and felt useful, maybe even happy. That's good; it's where your beloved would want you to be.

Know that your animal friend is fine now, and it's not your time to be with them. It hurts. Even as I write this three years later, I get a lump in my throat. But our lives are meant to go on. There is more life to live and other animals and people to love. This is not a platitude or a suggestion to rush out to get a new pet. That's for later. In the meantime, your beloved pet will wait for you to join them far in the future. Because they are the Best.

Acceptance

We don't "let it go" or "leave it behind".
Eventually, we must "move on" while carrying the load,
which, over time, gets lighter and lighter
until it is a butterfly on our shoulder.
Ever-present but just a wisp of a reminder
of the love cradled in our heart.

It amazes me that I wrote the above paragraph less than one month after Bryn died. I was still in shock, but on some level, I knew I would survive and be okay. Then, I was experiencing acceptance, although I did cycle back into sadness again later.

Acceptance gradually replaces depression, and we feel the pain less. This is the final stage for some, but hopefully not for you.

What does acceptance look like? It's the ability to grasp the truth of the loss without arguing, blaming, or feeling bereft. This could take a while. There may still be blame that's perfectly appropriate to lay somewhere. Perhaps someone was negligent. Perhaps someone was even purposefully hurtful. In that case, there's an entirely different level of recovery to be worked through.

So, even though you're in the acceptance phase, it may still be realistic and healthy to say, "If that driver hadn't run the stop sign, I could have caught the dog in time." The driver who ran the stop sign did something wrong and was negligent. They may be to blame, technically. Theoretically, though, the pet could have run out at a place where there wasn't a crosswalk or stop indicator. We need to accept that a terrible thing happened. We've lost something; it's broken us, and we'll do whatever we can to never let that happen again.

In the acceptance stage, the good memories begin bubbling up. We remember how caring the vet staff was. We can watch videos of the puppy playing in the sprinkler, and instead of sobbing, we chuckle. It doesn't mean our heart isn't broken or that we're "over it". It means the bleeding has stopped, and our hearts are starting to stitch back together. We see the light in the distance once again. We know we will survive this. Grieving doesn't mean that life is over, or that you never feel joy; there is just a missing piece – a little wag that should be there and isn't.

During the summer of 2019, I remember one time when I laughed out loud. It was sudden, a full-throated chortle that caught me by surprise. Our neighbor had made a random quip, nothing monumental. But for one clear second, I remembered. I remembered the way to joy.

There is no "getting over" grief, and those who think that's how it works or that's what we should do likely haven't experienced the kind of loss we're dealing with. Fortunate for them.

During the acceptance stage, we can go to the pet supply store without crying. We can snuggle other people's pets and young children without fear of breaking down. It doesn't mean we're not wistful sometimes. Even now, almost four years later (four years!) I get sniffly reading some of my journal entries from that dark summer. The feelings all come crashing back. Heck, hardly a writing session spent with this book goes by without me getting a little teary. It doesn't mean I've moved back into the depression phase; it's a pretty normal reaction to the memory of a traumatic event. Sometimes, it makes me sad remembering how sad I was.

One author mentioned being able to feel the loss of a childhood pet some 20 years later. She could be brought to tears at the memory of her Best Dog Ever. She'd had other wonderful pets over the years, but this Best Dog was seared into her heart. You and I understand this. She's not weak or crazy or in need of therapy now. She's firmly in the acceptance stage, possibly even to the point of finding meaning. However, she can still feel all the feels under the right conditions.

During this stage of the grieving process, you may begin considering bringing another fur baby (or feather baby) into your fold. If you feel ready, I say go for it. After Bryn passed, people close to me hesitated to ask if I'd get another pug puppy. I never even considered otherwise. How could I deny myself the joy and love I'd known once already? Of course, I wasn't ready to jump into a new relationship right away.

Of course, we shouldn't rush out to get a "replacement" comforter, especially if it's been a sudden or traumatic death. We need to get through the stages and be healing and settled in our acceptance of the current reality. If your pet was aged or suffered from a long-term illness, planning for a new companion may comfort you and provide something sweet to look forward to. Go for it. However, keep in mind that no two pets are alike, even if they are the same breed and sex (golly, don't I know it!).

To me, the benefits of loving our creatures far outweigh the fear of inevitable loss. *Here* is where I trot out the platitude, "It's better to have loved and lost than never to have loved at all." Loving – and losing – is living, and what is this life for, if not for living? This may sound like a hard sell. "Go out and open your heart up! Lay it down to get stomped on again!" If you're not ready, don't do it. It will be too hard on you and not fair to the new pet. It isn't disloyal or selfish to want a new companion in your life. You may be saving a life – or two (yours *and* the animal's). But only when you're ready.

When you feel ready, it may be appropriate to talk with your pet's healthcare provider about how things could have gone differently. This could help to avoid similar situations in the future with you or another client. If the situation was unavoidable, then this type of discussion might only bring up bad feelings and not help anything. In that case, I would try to dissuade you from airing your grievances with the vet. Although it might be helpful to the vet (and you) if you told them why you're taking your pets elsewhere (if you are), you are under no obligation to do so. It should go without saying that writing disparaging and/or vague reviews on internet review sites is rarely helpful for other pet owners or the vet. Typically, it's just a way for reviewers to carry out a grudge (warranted or not) without actually working toward a solution.

When we know we are in the acceptance phase, we may begin searching for meaning in our pet's death, or even in their life. Is it possible to find meaning after a tragedy and heartache? Yes, many have found meaning following the hardest times of their lives. Finding meaning is the final stage, as identified by David Kessler, and we'll talk about this in the next section.

Finding Meaning

Last night while walking to the camp showers, I looked up.
Guess what I saw. Yes, stars. More stars than I've ever seen before.
The longer I watched, the more stars became visible to me.
Shyly, they waited, seeing if I'd pay attention long enough
to make it worth their while to shine. I waited.
Soon, it was a sea of stars.
Each one lighting its own bit of the darkness.
It reminded me I am small, and my concerns,
though important to me, are not confounding the universe.
It gave me hope. The people, loves I've lost – they're not truly lost.
They're waiting somewhere out there.
Patiently waiting for my vision to expand so that I can see them.

Our broken heart will never be the same, but it will grow back together stronger, like scarred skin knit together. We have lost something we can never get back. But just because something is irreplaceable, does not mean that another equally valued thing won't make its way into our life at some point. To lose means you've loved, and if you've loved once, you can love again down the road.

Loss can do one of two things. Each loss can make our heart smaller, shrinking in on itself for protection like a snail being poked, retreating, backing farther from the light. Or it can make our heart grow – sometimes as big as the heavens. Because that's where our heart is now — in heaven. It can grow big enough to touch the stars and even to wrap around other people who've lost loves too. It's our choice – shrink or stretch.

Grief expert, teacher, and author David Kessler worked with Elisabeth Kubler-Ross on her classic research and writing of *On Death and Dying*. The five stages that modern culture has embraced as the stages of grief were originally identified within the population of the dying. After they wrote *On Death and Dying*, Kubler-Ross and Kessler wrote *On Grief and Grieving*. In the second book, they dove into the stages further as they apply to those who may not be dying, but grieving some other loss. Kessler later identified a sixth stage that he named Finding Meaning.

Can we find meaning in the loss of a loved one? Some people have, and of course many people haven't. I suppose it's just like all the stages. Not everyone will experience them all, and ineffective grieving may leave someone stuck in a stage without fully healing. When I say ineffective grieving, I'm referring to grief that never moves the suffering person forward; they never get to a place of peace or healing.

If we're writers or do other creative work, we can use our true past to create our art. It's one of many ways we move toward the final stage of finding meaning.

I believe pain allows us to know God better by drawing near to Him for comfort or being grateful to Him when pain is relieved. A pain-free life is the easiest way to take God for granted and leave Him in the background of our life.

One morning in early August 2019, I woke up with the words to the praise song *Your Love Never Fails* running through my head. As I sang the words that tell me He loves me, I wondered, "Does He love Bryn?"

We must decide for ourselves. Either God doesn't exist, and it's all random, or God exists. If He does, either He is unreachable and doesn't care, He is a vengeful God, or He is a loving God.. Considering babies, flowers, butterflies, sunsets, sunrises, breath in our lungs, chocolate, coffee, puppies, lions, the oceans, and on and on, I must decide. Are these mistakes and coincidences? Is color just a happy accident? I choose to believe that babies and other immeasurable gifts are not flukes of nature, but the physical manifestation of a loving Creator.

Coincidences and luck have never been part of my belief system. Everything is for a reason. If you're familiar with Gallup's Clifton Strengths, I rate high on Connectedness, meaning I believe and look for the connection between all things.

So for me, painful as it's been, I believe there is a reason for my loss. Perhaps this book is part of the meaning. Certainly, my compassion for others who've lost beloved pets and people has increased exponentially. So, with all of that, I believe God loves Bryn *and* me. He made her. He is all-knowing. I am not.

Perhaps faith is not your thing, and you believe in living day-to-day. You can definitely still find meaning in this significant loss. Your pet's life had meaning. You knew great love and joy. That is valuable. Some people find meaning by helping others or building personal growth in other directions. It may take time, but I believe that if you seek it, you will find meaning in your loss.

I have a theory that death brings life into sharper focus. If we allow it, death can open our hearts and minds to the possibilities, actually bringing us closer to the living. Lights are brighter; the beauty of a fluttering butterfly is more apparent. When pain sears our heart, we seek the gentle, the lovely, the true. Tears of grief cleanse our eyes so we can see what really matters.

We're going to be working out the death of a loved one our entire life. As we reach different stages and phases and circumstances, we'll see it differently and we'll have to come to grips with it in new ways. Hopefully, it will be easier each time we confront the loss, but it's just another rung on the ladder to healing. And like climbing a ladder, it's almost more effort to stay in one place, hanging on. That upward momentum carries us toward wholeness.

In the spring of 2023, my mom's closest friend unexpectedly became ill and died within two months. It was a brutal loss for her family and friends. As my mother compared it to the sudden passing of her sister years earlier, it gave me pause for thought. I believe that when someone you love dies, heaven's door opens just enough to let some light through. The more loved ones who travel through the door, the wider the crack becomes. If we're paying attention, at some point it's wide open for us, and we're prepared to walk through. Death is no longer scary; the unknown feels familiar because so many of our loved ones are there on the other side.

I hope that someday you will see the sliver of light from where your beloved pet left the door open a crack, and it will warm your heart knowing they are waiting for you.

My Story

us we were golden
the kind blessed beyond measure
or so it would seem

Longing

Losing a little dog inspired me to write this book, and the road to getting her was long and winding. Like so many of our stories, this one has its roots in my childhood. Most of my growing-up years, I lived in apartments and was raised primarily by a single parent. My mom is also not a big animal person, so all those factors combined into us being lucky if we had anything other than a fish. Still, I consistently dreamed about having a dog from a young age. Really, it was a fantasy.

As a childhood bookworm and library rat, I checked out lots of books. Mostly I read fiction, but when I chose a nonfiction book, it was about dogs. Obviously, having a dog was out of the question. In my dream state, I decided that whenever I finally got a dog, I knew exactly what I wanted. "I want a pug." Why? Who can know? And since I had about as much chance of getting a pug as getting on a space shuttle to Mars, no one asked why. Perhaps it was the pug's thick, compact stature (I was not a skinny kid), or perhaps it was their flattened nose and expressive eyes.

It's been postulated that one reason pugs are so popular is because their face resembles that of a small child. They look at you with those big, widely spaced eyes and cock their head to hear your words better. What's not to love? Anyway, I wasn't interested in any other dogs, and when there's no chance of getting it, you might as well dream big (figuratively speaking).

There came a time when I was 10 years old when I got a dog. We moved into a house, and my mom gave in. I had him for a few months, but I did not take care of him the way he needed. If you give an inexperienced 10-year-old full responsibility for a dog that's not allowed in the house, expecting them to train it and everything else, it will not go well. In the end, I had to return him to the shelter.

The loss, grief, and guilt I experienced related to those events shaped me in ways no one could know. That was my first experience with longing for, loving, and losing a pet.

Swiftly moving ahead to when I was more responsible and in control of my living situation, I lived with and loved several cats (mostly lovely) and several dogs (all fantastic). I've shared a home with a tuxedo cat, a tabby, a ginger cat, a tortoiseshell calico, and a black cat. They were all pretty nice, except that last one, who allows us to dwell in her home and pet her occasionally. We've mostly had mixed-breed dogs: German Shepherd mix, black Lab mix, King Charles Cavalier mix, then the pugs. We rescued the mixed breed dogs, one way or another, and solidly installed them as family members as our kids grew up. I grieved for their passings and miss each one.

I talk, talk, talk to her
She looks at me with eyes
So big, so expressive
She knows what I'm saying
Right?
Tell me she does
I hope
She does

Loving

Except for the pugs, most of the family pets I've mentioned experienced military life with us. They all endured at least a couple of moves (often cross-country) and were constant participants in a life lived on the road.

Finally, in 2017, when Paul retired from the Army, we settled in the Pacific Northwest – the region of my birth. Soon after that we deposited Ava, our youngest child, at university. Our pet companions were a middle-aged King Charles Cavalier Spaniel mix named Lucky and the black cat named Lola, who was in her prime. We must have experienced a somewhat typical empty nest syndrome, coupled with having a little more financial freedom. Whatever it was, something in the water made Paul say, "Maybe it's time you got that pug you've always wanted."

I didn't think he was serious. Well, I knew he was serious, but I didn't think it would actually happen. Get a dog from a breeder? Pay money for a dog when we'd always gotten perfectly wonderful dogs for free? Half of them had found us. A puppy now?

Of course, only whacko people raise their kids and successfully release them into the world, and then bring in a baby. Because if you didn't already know, I'll tell you. A puppy is a baby. I'm willing to die on this hill. You're up every two hours to take it out to train it to potty. It needs special food.

You can't leave it alone. You're not supposed to let it get near other dogs for a couple months to keep it safe from germs. Okay, it's not a human baby, but when you're in your 50's, it's far more exhausting getting up several times a night than it was in your 20's with that human baby. Just saying.

Paul tracked down a breeder online somehow. After we completed a detailed questionnaire, the breeder added us to her waiting list for a brindle girl. The brindle coat is the beautiful, stripy kind. This pattern is more commonly seen in Boxers and Great Danes, but occurs occasionally in pugs. We were at the end of a long waiting list, which is one indicator that the breeder is good and reputable.

If a breeder can meet you next week in a shopping mall parking lot with a puppy, beware. That's a clear sign of a puppy mill, which is bad all the way around – for the dogs, for you, for responsible breeders. Kayte was part of a network of pug breeders whom she trusted and would recommend. One of her breeder friends had a female coming into heat soon, and we got on her list for a brindle female as well. Brindle female (and male) pugs are rare and usually more expensive, but we figured "what the heck" – we'd try it.

The joining "took", and Misha (pronounced MEESH-kuh – Russian, for *Little Bear*) was pregnant by Davidson. With two gorgeous black pugs for parents, the pups could be any color. Misha's pregnancy was smooth and worry-free. The puppies were due in late July.

That summer, I spent a week volunteering in the kitchen at our church summer camp. The first Sunday I was there, July 22, 2018, I got a text that Misha was panting and refusing food, typical signs of beginning labor. I was so excited, and I prayed for all healthy babies. I shared my excitement with everyone else working in the camp kitchen like a kid at Christmastime.

After several hours, another text came saying Misha had delivered six perfectly healthy pups, and one was a brindle girl. So, we prepared to pay the higher brindle fee and waited to meet our new baby.

We'd already decided on the name Bryn, which means "high" in Irish. Similarly, the name of Bryn Mawr College in Pennsylvania means "high hill". So, our *high one* was born.

Two weeks later, we got to meet Bryn. She looked black, but in the right light her fur showed some striations. At that point, she was just a bug. We could hold her in one hand, and she weighed less than half a pound. Barely walking and still nursing 100%, she was a furry little bean. I was completely smitten. Misha, the mother, sat in the crib with the other five pups, watching me hold her baby. Other than running out to go potty or get a drink, Misha was a completely devoted mama.

As the late summer days tripped by, I made the two-hour drive to visit at least every other week until Bryn was eight weeks old. We would sit on the floor while six big head puppies toddled around us, peeing on the rug while pulling on our pants legs and sneaker ties. Mama Misha perched on the couch, watching us all with an eagle's eye. Laughing and cooing at the silly fur puffs, I took photos and videos just like a new mama or grandma would.

The weeks flew by. On our way home from one visit, Paul and I stopped at the Fred Meyer we passed in Sue's rural town. On the shoe clearance rack, I found a gorgeous pair of short velveteen flowered boots. Never having seen any like them before, I had to have them. Although I love those boots, it was years before I wore them again after losing sweet Bryn. I guess they always will remind me of her.

I look back on those joyous sunny days of pre-puppy loss and pre-pandemic life and think about how relatively *naïve* I was. As we all know, events would occur that most of us didn't even *know* could happen. Traumatic events often act as time markers in our lives. There is the *before* us and the *after* us. Thumbing through photos and remembering my singing heart during that time, it seems as if I was like a child who is lucky enough to have no idea how harsh the world can be. If you look at photos of yourself before and after a difficult time, is there a *knowing* in your eyes in the after pictures, even if you're happy and things are okay now? We've grown up in a sense, haven't we? Although we can experience sweet joy, we now know that coin has another side. We don't get to decide when it's flipped, and we surely don't get to choose heads or tails.

The September weekend Bryn came home, our daughter Ava, six hours away at college, came home for two nights to help me pick Bryn up.

Because of a pre-scheduled event, Sue met us halfway, so we didn't have to drive the full two hours with the puppy. Sue had wrapped little Bryn in a towel and kept her in a cardboard box. As military veterans and ROTC cadets milled around between exercises, Sue handed her over to me. I guess the puppy was probably in shock – being away from her home and mother for the first time except for a couple of vet visits. Knowing my scent from the visits and sleep shirt I'd left at Sues, Bryn snuggled right in, and we were on our way.

Although thankful for the shorter ride this time, I was sorry not to see Misha and the other pups for what I thought would be the last time. I didn't know that it's best for the mama to not see her puppies leaving. Self-centered me didn't consider the mother's loss of her baby, even though the baby was mature enough to be separated. I wanted to love on Misha and thank her for sharing her baby, but it was not to be – then.

Comfortable and curious, Bryn spent the ride home climbing all over Ava, never whining or peeing.

Of course, Lucky and Lola were waiting at home to greet us. Lucky was completely unimpressed with the new ball of fluff. Only mildly interested, Lola sniffed Bryn without hissing. As Bryn grew, she and Lola became great friends and teasers, chasing each other around the house. Although barking some, Bryn never tried to bite Lola, and Lola never hit her with claws out. They just spent a lot of time scrambling up and down stairs and under beds until Bryn was big enough to jump on them.

Potty training was traumatic – for me, not for Bryn. It's not as if I hadn't been warned. Pick up any book on pug training and it will plainly say that pugs are particularly recalcitrant to potty training. It isn't that they're not smart; they just don't care and are very stubborn. I've heard more than one animal professional assert pugs are some of the smartest dogs they've ever known. In my limited experience, I agree. Just because they don't do what you say doesn't mean they don't know exactly what's going on. They're kind of like your spinster Great Aunt Edna. She drives everyone nuts with her own self-centered eccentric ways, but she will be at your bedside with cash in 15 minutes when she knows you have a need. You know who I'm talking about. We all have an Aunt Edna (or wish we did). Pugs are the Aunt Ednas of the dog world – marching to their own drummers, but completely with the program and endlessly devoted.

Even at 10 months, Bryn would still pee in random places, including on our bed if she got excited or too tired. I take much of the blame for this. Even after repeatedly reading about how difficult pugs are to potty train because they are as stubborn as they come, I thought she would just "pick it up". That did not happen, and Bryn was still not entirely potty-trained when she left us. I learned from that experience, and when the next puppy came into our lives, I was on it like a flea on a dog.

For me, it was all a joy, despite the frustration. After the stress of having two eye surgeries the previous year and difficulties with extended family, I basked in the sunshine of the furry bundle of life in our house. Bryn was a sweet comfort, and I felt she was a reward to me for the trials I'd endured.

As most pugs are, Bryn was a snorer, so after she could be alone at night, we moved her from our bedroom down to the laundry room, where she had free rein. Crating has never worked for us with our dogs, although I know many pet owners swear by it. I didn't start soon enough, and I don't enjoy being that regimented. She was comfortable in the laundry room, with her bed, a toy, and water available, plus the cat creeping in and out through the night to keep her company. We never heard her whine or bark; she just waited sweetly at the gate when we went to her in the morning.

Since Lucky was entering his golden years, and we had a puppy, we bought a dog stroller. I figured Bryn would ride in it until she was big enough to walk the distance, and it would keep her safe from other dogs. When Lucky got old, Bryn would walk and he could ride. Alas, we didn't get that much time with either of them. Bryn hated the stroller, either yipping the whole time, or peeing in it, or both, so we started walking her earlier than recommended. Eventually, Lucky's slow pace could not be reconciled with Bryn's be bopping down the sidewalk. When she was several months old, I began walking them separately.

Bryn loved people, especially Ava and my mom. Although timid with small children, when she saw Lucky leaning in for a snuggle and wagging his tail, she jumped on them as if to say, "Look at me! I'm here too!"

She was a joiner, not a watcher. Getting jazzed when I sang and danced. Bryn didn't want to be held. She wanted to prance along. We especially enjoyed Cher's song "Heart of Stone". After Bryn passed, I remember thinking that I did wish my heart was made of stone.

Obviously, Bryn was a welcomed joy in our home and family, and an answer to dreams and prayers. She was more than I had hoped for in a little pug dog. She charmed all who knew her, including the puppy trainer who called her a "delight" and the vet, who grinningly said, "She has so much personality!" That sums it up. She was a delight teeming with endless shining personality.

Fate has played its shell game.
I stand empty-handed.

Losing

We moved through Bryn's puppyhood in fine form. All was well (except for the bane of potty training). We had her spayed at six months, and I practically had to tie her down to keep her from chasing the cat and popping some stitches. The only anomaly the vet ever mentioned was that when they performed a dental examination, he noted that Bryn's teeth did not seem fully formed. He said it was like she didn't have adult teeth waiting to push out the baby ones. I do not know if this had any significance to the health problem she later encountered. We did not discuss again it.

May 2019 was perfectly fine and gorgeous. The Pacific Northwest weather was unseasonably clear and warmish. Ava had finished her first year away at college. Our son and daughter-in-law's new baby was settling nicely into the family. Paul was scaling down at work to reduce his stress and hours away from home. I hadn't had an eye surgery in over a year. We had Bryn.

Everyone came to our house on Sunday, May 26, 2019, for a Memorial Day gathering. We took lots of pictures with the baby and Bryn and everyone. We picnicked and walked to the park a block away. Our son, Aaron, chased Bryn around the backyard and wrestled with her. When she got tired, she came to hide behind me, but soon ran back to him for more play. In pictures from that day, she's usually sitting beside me or looking at the baby. She either loved that baby or was jealous. We were blessed with a wonderful family day.

On Monday, I drove Ava to the airport to fly to Peru for two weeks on a veterinary mission trip. We both buzzed with excitement about this new adventure for her. When I got home from SeaTac airport several hours later,

Paul said, "Bryn really must have missed you. She seems depressed; she's been in bed most of the day."

There she was, lying in Lucky's bed in the dining room, under the sideboard table. She wagged her tail as I kneeled to pet her, but she stayed in the bed. This was not her typical hyper self on my returning home.

"Oh, she must be tired. Yesterday was a big day; she didn't have much time to rest with all the people around." I left her alone.

But the next day, she didn't act any better. She walked slowly, and we wondered if she was missing Ava or if she'd been injured during the outside playing. We let her rest and kept watching her. On Wednesday, she was no better. She continued walking stiffly, didn't get excited, and just seemed depressed. Obviously, not typical behavior for a 10-month-old dog.

I'd look out in the backyard and watch her standing in the middle of the grass, doing nothing. Her breathing seemed a little labored, making her sound congested. I still walked her every day, but because she was so slow, I took Lucky with us. She stayed close to me, no longer exploring the trees and yards along our route or pulling ahead on the harness to grab sticks.

After three days of acting weird, we got her into the vet on Thursday. The vet found nothing wrong with her. Although there was no sign of injury, he prescribed an anti-inflammatory just in case, plus Benadryl – because maybe it was allergies. That weekend, she started walking tight circles in the backyard. At mealtimes, it was as if she forgot what she was there for. She would sometimes just wander away from her food. As any pug lover – heck, any *dog* lover – will attest, this is NOT typical pug behavior. I was clueless, not even considering the darkest potential causes of her actions.

The next week, I took her back for x-rays. This time the senior vet examined her as well, and still they found nothing wrong. Knowing what I know now, if the vets had been at all familiar with pugs and potential complications, they would have suspected the diagnosis by this point. I didn't have my online pug support groups then, so I didn't ask anyone if they had any ideas. I didn't even check with the breeder. She likely would have known if I'd told her, but I never thought of it until after Bryn had passed.

The veterinarian apparently never researched her symptoms: reduced appetite, walking in pointless circles (a clear sign of neurological issues), and a quieter disposition. Healthy young pugs normally have voracious appetites and are highly active. If he'd consulted or studied, it would have popped right up, I'm sure. Not that he could have done anything about it. The train was headed down the track, and all we would have been able to do was to prepare and care. There is no cure for Pug Dog Encephalitis.

A note about the circling: It is perfectly normal for dogs to make tight circles as they prepare to lie down or when they're sniffing something particularly interesting. So, please don't freak out! But if your dog is standing in the middle of the yard, not sniffing anything and walking in small circles for no apparent reason, take them in. Don't wait. It may be something else, but it needs attention, whatever it is.

Ten days after she began acting strangely, late on that Thursday night, I found Bryn on the laundry room floor on the opposite side of where her bed was. It was as if she was trying to get somewhere and didn't know where, or her legs gave out.

On Friday night, we brought her to bed with us. She peed in her sleep on our bed. It was days later that we realized she must have had a seizure and lost control of her bladder. She'd probably had a seizure on Thursday night too before I'd found her on the floor.

On Saturday (12 days in), Bryn refused to eat. I was hand-feeding her bits of dog food and cucumber dipped in ranch dressing. She'd eat if I fed her, but it was as if bending her head down to the food bowl was painful. She spent the day in her bed. Panicked, I watched her closely, but the vet hadn't found anything wrong, and my brain could not even make it to the idea that this was something terminal. I just kept waiting for her to turn a corner toward wellness. This is classic denial, by the way.

I witnessed her seizures for the first time that day. We called and got her in to the emergency vet in Vancouver, about 45 minutes away. They didn't observe her seizing, but the young woman vet said, "Go home and look up pugs and seizures online." She obviously knew what was happening and didn't want to be the one to tell us. The neurologist was coming to the emergency clinic on Monday, and the emergency vet said we should bring her back so the specialist could see Bryn. She added, "This is what you have pet insurance for." Had we paid for all her tests and care out of pocket, our costs would have been astronomical.

We took Bryn home Saturday night, freaked out, praying. Not to minimize the effectiveness of praying, but for me, that was one way the bargaining phase manifested itself. While I sat on our bed, holding the subdued puppy, Paul searched for pugs and seizures online. "You should read this," he said.

"No. I don't want to."

He knew. I must have known. We didn't say anything else about what he found online. That's denial. I just held Bryn, while texting the family to pray and begging God for her to be better.

On Sunday morning, I stayed home from church with her. Lying under the sideboard table, in Lucky's bed, she wouldn't come out to eat or drink. She would only eat what I hand-fed her. While Paul was at church, Bryn started seizing again. I texted him, and he came home early. Again, we called the emergency vet in Vancouver and headed back down.

On Interstate 5, I sat in terror in the backseat with her. Updating the family, I again asked for prayers. Then, I texted a writer friend and fellow animal lover Stephanie, telling her about my broken heart. I knew she would understand. "You've given her the best that could be given," was all she could say. There were no promises or guarantees anyone could offer.

When we checked in, the vet tech came out to get Bryn. He asked me to describe the seizures. Paul was holding her, and I saw she was trembling like a leaf, but he hadn't felt it. Maybe his heart was thrumming too hard too. "She's doing it now," I said, and the tech immediately took her in the blanket we'd brought. That was the last time either of us held her.

Silently, we sat in the spacious waiting room while alert cats and dogs moved in and out before us. A dog that survived being hit by a car, left with only a damaged leg. An older lady who'd handed the tech her cat sat alone, quietly crying. I was too numb to even think about comforting her. After about 20 minutes, they let us know they were going to keep her for monitoring until the neurologist could see her Monday morning. Then we went back to say goodbye. Lying quietly in the empty spacious cage, Bryn sported a falsely cheery red velvety bell collar that would alert them when she was seizing. When we said goodbye, she didn't lift her head, wag her tail, or whine.

The rest of the day was rotten. Late in the afternoon, our church was having a picnic with canoe rides at the park. We walked the two blocks and stood around in the group, eating a piece of pizza. Paul stayed to chat; I went home, having spoken to virtually no one. I couldn't interact and just wanted to be alone.

At 11:00, we were in bed. Soon after we turned out the lights, my phone rang. It was the emergency vet, one whom we hadn't met. I put the phone on speaker.

"Bryn is becoming less responsive," he said. "We don't see this changing course. I'm calling to ask if you would like for us to euthanize her to end any suffering."

Choking, I said, "Yes," without even checking with Paul. I knew what he would choose.

"All right," said the vet, quietly. "Will you hold while I get the consent paperwork?"

"Yes," I whispered, tears streaming unchecked.

In less than a minute, he was back on the phone. "I'm sorry. Bryn expired while we were on the phone. The paperwork isn't necessary."

I broke into a million pieces and sobbed on Paul's chest.

The vet was still on the phone. I got back on, sniffling. "Would you like to come see her?"

"No," I said.

Paul said, "Are you sure?"

I looked at him. I wasn't sure. "Yes," I said to the phone. "We'll be there in a while."

We got dressed in scruffy clothes, and I grabbed a stuffed pug I kept for overnight trips away from home. Somehow, I knew I'd need something to hold on to on the ride home.

Less than an hour after Bryn had taken her final breath, we entered the main door of the emergency vet hospital. The lobby was dark and quiet. There may have been a client sitting in there, but I don't remember. The only person I remember was the receptionist, who got up and led us to a side door. Of course, she knew without us saying anything. Paul might have said, "We're here for Bryn." That we entered without an animal, and I probably looked like I'd been through the ringer, were sure giveaways.

The side room was low-lit and quiet. It was like a really boring living room, with a couch, a couple of soft chairs, end tables, and lamps. What struck me most were the many stacks of boxes of tissues. Tissue boxes filled the shelves, the open cupboards, and sat on every surface. I had the thought that perhaps we were, in fact, in a tissue storage room, not a waiting room.

We sat on the couch, silent.

After a moment, the vet came in from a different door. He was young – maybe they all are at the emergency vet hospitals. He introduced himself, offered his condolences, and said, "Do you have any questions for me?"

Paul said, "So, what was the final cause of death?"

The vet swallowed. "Most likely rupture of the brain stem."

I stared straight ahead. All those tissue boxes.

"It was quick. She did not suffer."

I wanted to say, "How could you possibly know?" But I wanted to believe him. Hopefully, she "died in her sleep".

"Stay as long as you like." He slipped from the room.

Right after, a tech pushed a wheeled cart into the room. Bryn laid on it, most of her body covered with a blanket, her head resting on her front paws as if she were sleeping. The bell collar was gone. I laid my hand on her back; she was warm. I never asked, but we assumed they put her on some kind of warmer while we were en route. I buried my face in her soft black fur, but she smelled like a hospital, not like herself.

The scene was ominously peaceful. The room, the lighting, the posed dog. We heard no sounds from outside. After all, it was after midnight. Everything felt swathed and gentle except for me. I had never cried so much in my life. I couldn't believe it. Those tissue stockers knew their clientele.

I took some pictures – of her, of us, of the tissue boxes. Weeping, I asked Paul, "What should I say to her?"

He barely hesitated. "Tell her she was a good dog. The best dog."

So I did.

We didn't stay long. After all, she was somewhere else now, and I could cry just as easily in the car. We thanked the receptionist and left.

That stuffed pug I'd brought did its job. I slept with it for weeks after that.

Bryn died on Sunday night. The next few days were a bizarre blur. On Monday, Paul was home from work. I spent the morning informing the family about what had happened, as well as informing Sue the breeder and her network. I emailed our regular vet and submitted the insurance claim.

I even emailed Bryn's first vet, the one who saw her as a tiny puppy. She had moved to a job in Portland months before. Within a day, she emailed back with her condolences. She had heard through the grapevine about a pug puppy that had died, but she didn't know it was mine. I found it intriguing that vets between two states had discussed the case.

The day was sunny and felt blazing hot. We walked to the Starbucks in Safeway to get out of the house and get a cold drink. Inside, we ran into a lady from church. While standing there acting normal and chatting about nothing, I thought, "How surreal this is. I am mourning my dead puppy and having this mundane conversation." I didn't say, "You know my dog just died. My puppy. My love." It was all wrong – the weather, the conversation. It should have been raining like tears.

Ava was to fly back from Peru the next day. We'd talked a few times while she was gone, but we hadn't chatted that weekend. I wanted her to know about Bryn before she came home. So, I texted her it was bad news about Bryn. Ava wanted to FaceTime. As I relayed the events of the weekend, dry-eyed, I watched my typically stoic girl a continent away, swiping at tears. It was probably better that she hadn't been home to see me at my worst. It was also good for me she was coming home now.

Less than a week later, the emergency vet office called to tell us Bryn's remains were ready. The three of us drove down to Vancouver, bringing a big box of See's candy for the staff with a note thanking them for their kindness during our ordeal.

One week after Bryn died, Lola the cat had a routine appointment. When I arrived at the vet's office and told them my name, the receptionist said, "So, this is Bryn?" Feeling a punch in my gut, I wanted to say, "Um, no. Bryn is a dog, and she's dead, and this is a very much alive cat." After a moment of stunned silence, I said, "No, this is Lola."

The response was, "It says she's dead." Someone had marked the cat in the computer as deceased instead of marking Bryn's record. It was a human mistake, but it never should have happened. Communication was so lacking within the office that only the vet knew my puppy had died that week because I emailed him. These are the types of things that were on my "sins of the vet" list, and they are issues that are completely avoidable.

No one at the office other than the vet acknowledged our loss. There was no card, no condolences from the staff, just business as usual. It was a little shocking, considering the practice of our previous vet in another state. In that office, when a family was saying goodbye to their beloved pet, a lit candle sat on the front desk with a note encouraging people to speak quietly and be respectful. That previous vet also sent us a condolence card when our cat Pumpkin died naturally at home. I didn't expect a candle, since they did not euthanize Bryn in the office. However, some sort of acknowledgment would have been appropriate.

I did feel a round of anger aimed at the vet office's thoughtlessness. Honestly, if we had lived in a larger city with more options, I would have changed vets at that point; the whole thing was so trying for me. But we didn't live in a larger city, and I didn't see another vet. Life goes on. Then the pandemic happened, and, well, you know. We were all just trying to survive.

Some people help us ride out the course of our grief. They listen without judgement, regardless of whether they understand our feelings. They don't question, don't push us to hurry up and smile, or clean up that pet stuff in the corner. My extended family blessed me by being sweet, even those who didn't really understand (aka the non-animal people). They knew the loss was huge for me, regardless of how they felt about it.

Then there are the people who aren't helpful. The least helpful person I encountered during my time of deep grief was the woman who, at a social gathering, after I told her my puppy had died the previous month, spent the entire time talking about the dog she lost years ago, yammering on. How much she loved that dog, what a great dog it was, how it died, etc.

I understand now that she needed to process her feelings. Perhaps she wasn't given space at the time for her grief, or she didn't know how much it had affected her until I shared my loss. Simply put, though, it was not the time for her to share. What I needed was someone quiet who listened and nodded and said, "I know how hard it is. I'm so sorry." That's all.

In contrast, it blessed my heart the week after Bryn died, when Paul took me to a large camping event. (No, that wasn't the blessing!) Although I am not a camper, I went along to get a change of scene, and it was near a great little town, Leavenworth, WA.

Two encounters on that two-night trip brought me some comfort. The first was on the main street of Leavenworth. A man was walking his pug along the sidewalk. I asked to pet his dog, and the man and I chatted a bit. Pugs are not that common (don't let the greeting card industry fool you); you just don't see them on the street that often, so this was a shining light for me. I don't think I told him about Bryn.

On the second day, as I sat in a camp chair at our site, Paul arrived. "There's someone I want you to meet." I followed him along the periphery of the large camp area until we reached a big, old truck-bed camper. Through the back window, a dog we could hardly see yapped at us. When Paul knocked on the door, a pleasant-looking middle-aged woman opened it.

"I brought my wife to meet your dog."

The woman didn't even have to call the dog; she ran to the door. At the top of the steps stood a little old fawn (that's the most common brown and black pug coloring). This little lady wore a pink tutu. Other than graying in her face and thickening around her middle, she was young at heart, friendly and active. The woman told us, "She's 13. My husband and I had four boy children. She's my girl." The visit made my day, and it lifted my spirits to think I could walk around the corner and at any second see that sweet pug.

After Bryn died, it was months before I could go to the pet supply store. It was a coup for me when I could walk into that store without tearing up. Perhaps for you it's a route you always walked with your dog, or even the grocery store, if you took your dog in or left them in the car while you shopped. It may be difficult to be around other people's pets or small children during this time, because they remind you of your own little one. Don't push yourself into going places that will be difficult. You'll know when you're ready. It's okay to walk a different route, shop at a new store, or order your groceries for a time.

For a few weeks after Bryn's death, I avoided visiting my toddler granddaughter, whom I typically saw every couple of weeks. I stayed away a little longer because my grief was so fresh, I was afraid something about this small, snuggly, dependent creature would remind me of what I'd lost, and I would break down and possibly upset the baby. Of course, I had no idea if that would really happen, but I had that fear, so I took a brief break. Alternatively, sometimes being near little ones or other animals can be very comforting for the grieving person. Do what makes you most comfortable during this time.

Through all of this, what none of us could know then was the incredible blessing of timing. Although Bryn's time was far too short, it was only nine months later that the world shut down with a pandemic. During her many vet visits, there were no limits to how many people could be in the vet office or for how long. Our sweet dog Lucky passed in 2022, and even though we had to wear masks, they still allowed us inside with him. What an additional trauma to have to say goodbye through a glass door. I'm so sorry for those who've had to endure that.

I've come a long way since that fateful summer of 2019, but I still grieve, especially as I worked on this book. This is normal, and whether you lost your pet last week or 20 years ago, the pain may sometimes hit you again. It's a process, and grief is like an uncontrollable sea; sometimes calm and cradling, other times threatening to wash us overboard and drown us.

I'm very thankful for the advice of Bryn's first vet, who examined her as a perfectly healthy tiny puppy. "I suggest getting pet insurance," she said.

"These dogs can get expensive." She was right. Not only with Bryn, but our other pugs as well. However, even mutts (often considered the least risky for health problems) and run-of-the-mill house cats (I know *none* of our kitties are run-of-the-mill) get serious illnesses. If you can afford it, pet insurance can offer some peace of mind. There are several reputable companies in the field.

Wherever you are on your journey, I highly recommend pet insurance – especially if your pet is young with a long life expectancy, or if it's a breed known for complications. For us, this coverage lessened the sting of that last very expensive weekend of Bryn's life. It also gave us the freedom to say to the vet, "Do everything." What a painful situation to be in: making healthcare or end-of-life decisions for any loved one with a calculator in your hand. You have my sympathy, if this has been the case with you. Sometimes, we simply can't afford what it's going to cost, and we must make excruciating choices. I'm so sorry.

Be aware that care plans through specific vets or pet store chains are not insurance. Insurance covers unexpected (and occasionally routine) costs. Care plans (or pet wellness plans) are prepaid, often discounted programs to ensure regular appointments and care, such as routine vaccinations and examinations.

It feels as if I've been holding my breath since Bryn died,
And now I can let that breath out.
There are still stressors and fears and work and worries.
But the weight on me has mostly lifted.
I can walk by her memory stone and feel joy, not sorrow.
It's a blessing to watch Bridget blithely patter
Across the ground in front of Bryn's stone,
Completely clueless about what we've been through.
As Bryn smiles over us, I feel her say, "You go, little sister. You go."

Living Again

How do we live again once acceptance has come to stay? Of course, it's different for every person. Maybe we find we can think about our pet fondly, without tears or bitterness. Hopefully, we've arranged the memorabilia we've kept in a way that comforts us rather than causes us sadness.

Rituals are important. All cultures have rituals to commemorate and honor the dead, as well as supporting the living through their loss and grief. We can do the same with animals. The rituals can be as simple or as complex as you like.

I scrapbook pages or entire books (depending on how many memorabilia I have for the pet) for each animal who's shared their life with our family. These creatures are part of my children's heritage. They were integral parts of our family at different stages and in different places. Their presence immeasurably enriched our lives. The photos and scrapbooks help us all remember these gifts.

Scrapbooking may not be your thing. However, there are many ways to honor and commemorate our pets' lives. For our last two pets that have passed (Bryn and Lucky), we've chosen cremation. We are blessed to have a wonderful local company that provides the service of creating a paw print, saving a lock of fur, and sealing the ashes in a beautiful box with the pet's name on it. You can choose something such as this as part or all of your memorial ritual.

Now that we're living in a permanent location, I also memorialize the pets in our backyard. I commissioned an engraved stone with Bryn's birth and death dates that sits by a rosebush I planted just for her. For Lucky, we ordered a colorful metal sun and had his dates engraved on a shiny blue plaque that hangs below the sun. From the fence, Lucky's items watch over Bryn's stone and rose bush in the sunniest space in our yard. Bryn (like many pugs) and Lucky recharged by lying in the sun, spending as much time as possible basking in its rays. It's a pleasant way to remember my two sunspots.

There are so many ways you could memorialize your pet in your yard or on a balcony, porch, or patio. Plants, statues, birdbaths, and wind chimes are lovely possibilities. If you move frequently, choosing something portable is a great idea.

Sharing the news of your loss with family and loved ones can be a ritual too. People who care about you will want to know, and it reduces the chances of awkward questions later on such as, "Where is Danny Boy?"

I've recently learned of a practice called a "wing walk". A person chooses a path, loop, or favorite walking route of the deceased, and routinely (it could be daily; it could be yearly) walks that path communing and conversing with the departed one. I think that's a beautiful tradition that one person could have, or the whole family could share.

Right after Bryn died, I found one of the first photos we had of her in our house – she was probably less than 12 weeks old in the photo. I had it printed and enlarged to an 8" x 10" and placed on a hard backing. This picture stands on Paul's desk in our bedroom. It doesn't make us sad. She was happy, healthy, and we were thrilled at the time that picture was taken. Pictures – singles or montages – are excellent memorials.

Whatever makes you and your family comfortable is okay. Forget about what people who don't live in your home think. It's your home, your grief, your healing. I'm sure you don't go and tell them what you'd prefer them to display in their homes!

Donating to animal charities is a wonderful way to commemorate your pet. You could do this annually or give a onetime gift in your pet's name. When Paul's aunt lost her therapy dog, we donated to the dog rescue she loves so much. Being in another state, I've never been to that rescue. It wasn't my dog, but contributing in sweet Andy's name made everyone feel just a little better.

How do you know you're ready to love again? Some clues are: 1. You're not crying your eyes out on a regular basis. 2. You can think about your beloved without becoming melancholy or morose or crying – at least sometimes. 3. You find yourself thinking about how nice it would be to have another furry body running around the house, or lounging about, or snuggling with you. 4. You meet a new animal that you feel a connection with, and you wonder if you two would be a good fit.

No one can tell you when it's the right time. It may take a month; it may take a year. Enough time should elapse so that you're not comparing the two animals too often. Of course, we always compare our pets, just like we discuss the differences between our children. That's completely natural. "Zooey liked that dry food, but Scooter will only eat this brand." Or "Mr. Wigglesworth would only eat while sitting on the counter – what a diva, but little Thor will eat anywhere!" They all have their quirks and personalities, just like people.

If we're expecting the same kind of love, reactions, and habits from a new pet as a previous one, we're not quite ready. Because they really do have their own personalities. We have owned three female pugs, and they are each very different. All have been spaz (I think pug owners invented the word zoomies), as well as incredibly loving, active, and smart. But one's a barker, one's super clingy, one was pretty chill. Oh, to have only calm pets. We've had a dog that heard the thunder before we did and panicked, and we have one now who I think you could set off every smoke detector in the house, and she would simply cock her head in wonder. Have I mentioned they're all different?

When you are ready for another animal to rescue you, you'll know it. You'll feel the itch. "Let's go to the shelter," you'll say. You'll find yourself perusing the breeder's website or looking for puppies in the paper. Although I currently have purebreds, I have almost always adopted rescues and strays. I fully support the "adopt, don't shop" movement. Pet stores that sell non-rescued animals are often supporting puppy mills and unscrupulous breeders – knowingly or unknowingly. Really, there's no excuse for not knowing by now. Also, there is anecdotal evidence that mixed-breed dogs tend to be healthier because there's a lower "concentration" of the same genetic defects. Being a pug mix might have saved my Bryn.

I had the opportunity to prepare for a new love not long after Bryn's passing. Just a couple of weeks after she died, our breeder contacted me that Bryn's mother, Misha, was expecting again. She offered me another puppy for free, saying that the father had tested negative for the PDE gene. We accepted her offer without hesitation. The puppies were due in late August 2019. So, as I grieved Bryn's passing, I had a new puppy to look forward to. It was an odd experience because I really wanted Bryn back. Although the anticipation surely helped my healing, as well.

Sue invited me to Misha's delivery in August, and I made it there in time. I got to be the first person to hold Bryn's half-sister, Bridget. Cradling that sweet newborn pup was key in my ability to transition from depression to the acceptance phase of grief. Our Bridget is that frisky girl who trots in front of Bryn's memorial stone and eats grass under Lucky's sun.

When we got Bridget several months after Bryn's death, I told the breeder that when it was Misha's time to retire, we would take her. After all, she was the mother of both of my pug babies and a sweet girl to boot. We thought we had a few years to wait for her, but Misha was retired early because of medical concerns. So, she came to us less than a year later. Apparently, in our family, if you lose one dog, you get two more. Be careful what you wish for. Regardless, these girls bring me happiness every single day, and there's joy in knowing I have Bryn's mama and sister here with me.

The anniversary of your pet's death can be a sweet time or a sad time. You may feel completely healed one year after your pet dies, or you may still tear up and feel the emptiness in the house. Neither end of the healing spectrum is wrong; it's just where you are. Commemorate the anniversary in whatever way is comfortable for you. If you want to raise a glass of bubbly to the memory of your pet or write to them in a journal entry about how you've fared in the past year, go for it. If you take advantage of the ideas shared later in the book to write, craft, and share about your beloved pet, a one-year anniversary may be a good time to look back through those records and see how far you've come.

When I looked back at some of my journaling and poems after several months or a couple of years, I was shocked by what a dark place I'd been in. Reading those passages made me sad for my former self, but it also made me proud of how I had made it through to a stronger, more compassionate place, with more wisdom. Losing Bryn brought me to a place of emotional growth and increased capacity to feel empathy for the pain of others. I've also learned that I'm strong in ways I'd never considered.

If it's too painful, don't go back. Those notes will wait – forever if necessary. This is something that's totally about you and your feelings and healing path.

Although I don't have any anniversary rituals, I make it a point to regularly visit the area in our backyard memorializing Bryn and Lucky. I like to make sure their plaque and stone are clean, in good shape, and the weeds aren't taking over, as gardening is not my strong suit.

If the anniversary passes by without you noticing, I would say that's a good thing. You are in a new phase of life that doesn't revolve around grief and the past. It's not disloyal to your pet. They would want you to live, not continue grieving.

How ever you choose to remember your pet, I hope it brings you joy and gratitude for what they gave you.

Poetry

All poetry and prose in this book are the original creations of the author.

Haiku

<u>Knife of Truth</u>
walking in a fog
until the knife of truth stabs
pain of loss breaks through

<u>Wondering</u>
oh Bryn – when will I
stop missing you and wond'ring
why you had to leave?

<u>July 2, 2019 (3 Weeks After)</u>
heartbreak shackles me
two days 'til Independence
will I be free then?

July 9, 2019
I remember how
everything stopped being fun
when Bryn said goodbye

July 10, 2019
my world darkened by
the shadow of a pug dog
whose love never ends

Cling
oh little pug dog
if I had known you'd leave me
I'd cling 'til the end

I Won't Say It
how to say goodbye
see you later I'll miss you.
you stay (in my heart)

Here's Hoping
someday, seeing your
picture will bring me joy not
sorrowful mourning

July 19, 2019
why do you haunt me
in quiet hours of night
when I miss you most

July 23, 2019
why can't you be here?
why are we separated?
please wait for me there

July 25, 2019
you can't escape hurt
it comes in so many shapes
concealed as a friend

Tactile Memory
caressing the pen
that you hid under the bed
after you chewed it

Useless Worries
you taken from me
I didn't see it coming
worry list too short

Saturation Point
catching me off guard
tears well up for no reason
missing you engulfs

New Resident
the tears come slower
anxious with loss my heart pounds
grief is here to stay

All the Wrong Places
it's been a rough day
you're in all the wrong places
which is everywhere

Dark Message
the nights are the worst
day quietly settling
whisp'ring that you're gone

Light and Dark
in dark I feel more
I fall asleep with lights on
sadness kept at bay

Inexperienced
I didn't know lack
had I known what I could lose
I'd hold on tighter

Uninitiated
those who've never lost
can't see the empty cisterns
inside the mourning

Silent
you don't know my pain
are you in my flesh on bone?
"til then keep silent

Hope
all my eyes can see
is a tiny speck of light
surrounded by dark

You Would Have Been a Year
we miss cake with you
taken from us too early
worst birthday ever

July 25, 2019
gloomy days drag on
I look for the sunny spots
all I see is you

Happiness is a Good Thing
good things come to me
I wonder if happiness
will come to me too

Poems

Strange Love
My wall-eyed beauty
Come closer, grunt into my ear.
Our love transcends life.

Wednesday (3 days after Bryn's passing)
The cat watches while I put your toys in the washing machine.
Then I let her sniff my hands.
We share your memory with our eyes.

Same Wednesday
I used to be tough, strong, impenetrable.
"Bring it on", I said. "Until I am dead, I will fight."
That was before you broke me.
The key to survival is knowing your own weaknesses,
As well as the enemy's.
How was I to know that my strength was my weakness?
How was I to know that love would be my undoing?
Someday (not today) again I will be strong.
And my weakness will again be my strength.

The Saddest Thing

The saddest thing is
That nothing smells like you
Not even your blanket.

Unsent Invitation

Standing alone, preparing dinner at the kitchen counter,
I wait to feel her push against my calf with a soft toy, inviting me to play.
The invitation never comes.

A Semblance of Normal

I'm dressed
Made up
Hair's in place
Bag packed
Ready to face the world
Or so it seems
But you're still not here.

Death

Will either stop you or spur you
Of course your own –
you know what that does
But another's?
Both fits and starts
backwards – forwards
Hold on
Dig in
Don't let go
Until you are spurred back to life.

Dear Onlooker

The worst is saying, "It's just a dog" and forgetting entirely
Or making it seem as if you've forgotten.
Being awkward, asking, hugging are all okay.
We all want to be remembered – for better or worse.
And for better or worse, I want to remember.

July 11, 2019

The tears don't come the way they used to.
I feel a cold numb.
My arms miss the heft of carrying you.
My fingertips miss your silk-soft ears,
the tight curl of your tail, your thick brindle fur.
I miss the physicalness, the matter of you.
But I'm told (and I believe when I'm strong) that
Your matter was simply a housing unit for your soul.
Your eternal, buoyant, radiant, loving, inquisitive soul.
The housing unit is reduced to ash. Still, silent, cold.
Like my pain and the emptiness in my chest
That waits for me every new dawn.

Normal – Not

I'm still sleeping with a stuffed replica.
Trying to figure out how to be normal, to be grateful.
I seem normal.
I'm sitting by myself, crying in bed.
I'm not normal.

<u>How Could it Be? (One month after Bryn's death)</u>
How could it be
One month
Since I held your warm body
Since I stroked your fur
Since I told you how I loved you and
Begged you not to leave me.
One month since I slipped off your collar for
The last time.
One month since Lucky and Lola have seen you.
They still smell you in places. I can tell.
One month.

<u>July 16, 2019</u>
You were a constant sunshine that used itself up.
Even the sun won't last forever.

<u>Gratitude</u>
Thank you for eyes
That cry real tears and a heart
That can feel real pain.
Thank you for skin
That feels the burn and the cut.
Thank you for ears
That hear the wail of the violin,
The new baby,
The grieving mother.

July 21, 2019

The unbearable weight of your absence
Fills the room with an empty clamor
That stretches its greedy fingers into every corner.

How Do You Say Goodbye?

How do you say goodbye
To 18 pounds that filled a room?
Everything was touched by her.
Even this journal has her chew marks.

Painted Carcass

Sarcophagus
So ornate, so pretty
Perfect on the outside
Empty as death

Ode to a Little Dog

Your time with us was so short.
As if you were a ghost passing through.
A dark gray wisp of love and matter
That wove around every cell of my heart.
Slicing it to ribbons as it passed on through
And moved away to higher climes.
I bleed still. Not such a hemorrhage as before.
But a seeping trickle.
Requiring just enough clean-up
To tear off the tenuous scab.

Holding the Pain

Holding it in
Pushing it down
From my mind
Eyes
Heart
In my stomach
It doesn't want it
It all comes out
Of my mouth
My eyes
My lungs
Rocking
My body doesn't want it
Neither does my soul.

The Dam

One small switch flicked
How are you
What happened
Tell me about it
I am so sorry
The deluge comes
It can't be helped.

Quarantined Heart

Can they see I'm not the same inside?
I never will be the person they knew.
Can I keep the façade, the brave face?
Or will the gray pain leak through my pores
Until they know I'm the ghost of past me?

Lifeless

Brushing my hair
Sharp intake of breath
Am I dying?
No, I already did
I am the walking dead
You only see the clear hemorrhage
From my eye.
Silent, stealthy, relentless
I won't bleed to death
Because the dead can't die.

Alone

Alone in my bed.
Alone in my house.
Alone at work.
Alone at the store.
Alone in a crowd.
Alone without you.
Alone in a world
Where I was never alone
As long as you were in it.

Burning

The world is full of sadness.
People seem to be vessels of flesh
Holding heartbreak, grief, disappointment.
The outsides are polished up and pretty.
But the insides burn with acid.

She Laid There, Like Sleeping

I found a dead squirrel yesterday
On the rubber mat on our front walkway.
It had been there maybe a day.
It was stiff. Only flies were around, nothing else.
I have no idea how it went. There was no sign of injury.
It just lay there, like sleeping.
(She laid there too, like sleeping.)

In Shadow

The shadow of a pug darkens my heart
Where once
That shape burst with sunshine.

Holograph

Since you've gone away, I'm an empty shell
I've lost myself since you finally fell
To outsiders, I look the same as always
But inside, my cries fill both nights and days
I operate near maximum level
Though my heart's lost its ability to revel
When you hear the sound of my laugh
Remember, I am just a holograph.

Scrolling

I keep scrolling through pictures of you.
Ordering more and more –
For scrapbooking, I tell myself.
As if that will bring you back.
Perhaps if enough tears fall on the photo paper,
Your picture will come to life,
And this will all be just a bad dream.

August 25, 2019

If I had known
That I would lose all trace of the smell of you
I would have inhaled and held it.
That I would miss the most irritating things about you
I would have embraced your very presence.
That sleeping with a stuffed version of you would have to suffice
I would have suffered through snoring.
That getting you and loving you
Would lead to the greatest hurt I've ever known.
I would have done it anyway.

Healing

What does healing feel like?
A scab that grows into a scar.
It doesn't bleed anymore
But the evidence remains of a cut so deep
Until the scar turns into a silver streak
That encapsulates a pain from the past.

Stuff I Wish I Didn't Know

"Broken heart" is a literal term.
Few others understand my pain.
I didn't understand the pain of others
Missing someone's smell hurts too.
A person can literally wake up crying.
Stuffed animals also work for grownups.
The true meaning of "walking wounded".
That so many of us are just that.
I can actually live without you.

Misha's Last Puppy

I've borne my last pup. He didn't survive.
It is time for my life to change.
I was a puppy, a bitch, a mama.
I will always be the second and third.
I have borne more than a dozen puppies;
Most have survived.
I've known a few males. Those relationships were brief.
I have loved my humans and been greatly loved.
I will now go to a new home,
With new humans who will love me.
And with one of my last puppies.
We will live and play and sleep together
Until the last of our days.
She is strong. She is brave. She is me.

Love Notes

July 16, 2019

To the woman I met while I walked my dog last year. I am sorry. We stopped to talk. You were breathless, perhaps even seeming manic, maybe just before tears. Walking a beautiful Golden Retriever, you told me about the dog you'd lost. Was it a day, a week before? I'm sorry, I don't remember, but I stood and listened politely. You told me how much you loved that dog and how you held him as he died, and you would only take your dogs to The Hill because they had the best vets.

I stood, listening, thinking you were a little crazy. Because you had never seen me before that day. But I walked my dog on the same street as you that morning.

It was cold. I remember how red your cheeks were, and I was amazed that your hands were bare (I always need gloves). They looked ruddy and thin and chapped. You were pouring out your heart, and you had on a red jacket, while our dogs waited patiently and sniffed each other, then stood quietly, puffing warm breaths above the frozen sidewalk.

I just didn't get it because you had that gorgeous dog you were walking. So, of course you must be recovered and fine now, right? That's what I thought after that moment, a year ago.

I don't remember your dog's name or when you had to drive him to Portland to be put to sleep and how recently that had been for you. I'm so, so sorry. If I ever see you again, I will ask about your dog and about you. And if you want, I'll give you a hug. For both of us.

Because now I understand.

July 16, 2019

Grab joy. You have to take it in your teeth and hold on. Run away when someone tries to take it from you. If you lose it, spend all your time searching for it. Never give up on joy. Sometimes you have to let love go – some things are just out of your control. But not joy. It's never best to let it go.

#lessonsmydogtaughtme

July 18, 2019

There's a hole in my heart. Sometimes people live with a hole in their heart for years. Eventually, when it's discovered, surgeons may close and patch it. The hole is gone, but there is still a scar.

In young children, sometimes the hole will grow closed as they mature. They are monitored for signs of distress, but often concerns dissipate. As in other things, the well-tended child has a greater chance of healing on their own than a broken adult does.

July 22, 2019

Today an email from the AKC reminded me it's your birthday.

July 28, 2019

In my basket of flip-flops, I have one without a partner. I know the partner is hidden somewhere in this house – most likely under a bed. Bryn was adept at stealing and hiding things. I have not searched for it; I don't need it. Someday, I will find it, accidentally, when Bryn is the last thing on my mind, and I'll have her back. For one brief moment, I will feel the fullness of the naughty puppy who destroyed more shoes than all of our other dogs put together, was relentless in her thievery, and never understood why anyone was frustrated with her. I will have the love that forgives all. A love that saves broken things to feel whole again.

August 20, 2019

Lord, thank you for cracking my heart open. I wasn't hard-hearted, but my heart was encapsulated, convenient, just fitting. Now my love oozes out, even streams, sometimes bubbles because my granddaughter grew it, and Bryn broke it. The precious oil of love and devotion cannot be recaptured. The container cannot be sealed. A heart can heal, but the beautiful scar will always remain.

Petco

Today I went to Petco for the first time since you died. I was dreading it. I had literally not gone into that store without buying a new toy (or two) for you in months and months. But I made it; I bought cat and dog food and walked by the toys without tearing up.

I hate that you're gone, and I would do or give up almost anything for you to be lying on the couch beside me, healthy, alive. I cannot rationalize the loss. Or even know the good. Romans 8:28 tells us that all things work together for good to them who love God, to them who are the called, according to His purpose. I don't know what good will come from this. One good thing I can think of now – that we only know you as a young, spry pup, so full of life. We never saw an old, broken-down Bryn. You are forever youthful — a perpetual puppy — in the arms of our Creator.

Death

We fight Death as if we could possibly win. Sometimes we win a battle, but we will not win the war. Sometimes, Death steps back and says, "Okay. Not now." We all know what that means.

But what to make of young death? The greatest philosophical and religious minds have not untangled that one. It's as if Death says, "I just wanted to remind you who's in charge here. Just a little humility check-in. Sometimes I step back, but I am never cheated."

Left Behind

I feel as if I've lost myself. Somewhere back there, the essence of me – has been left behind. I'm a shell. My heart is in a box on my mantle, and no matter how I work or dig or laugh, I'm a holograph. If I ever got you back, I would never let you go. I wouldn't leave you.

Tribe of the Grieving

I am rereading A Grief Observed by C.S. Lewis. So far, I'm crying continuously. I am part of a new family now – those who have loved deeply and lost. This is no broken love affair. This is the final parting on this earth. Only in heaven shall we meet again. I have been tried and initiated. I am a member of the tribe of the grieving.

Grateful

May every person be so lucky as to have the love I've received.

To Bryn

July 1, 2019

I am so much less afraid of dying now because I know you're there waiting for me.

July 5, 2019

Years ago, when the young child of a mutual friend passed away, my friend Tracie said to me, "Heaven is so much closer now." I thought I knew what she meant. Now I truly do. Heaven is just a step away, and when it's my turn, I'll run across with arms outstretched for you. You call to me, "The water is great. It will be when you come. Whenever you come."

July 23, 2019
You retaught me what it means to feel.

August 1, 2019
Dear Bryn,
Will we ever know why you left so soon? When we get to heaven, will it matter?

Everything I do, I think of you. You should be here. You should be underfoot, by the heater, begging for a carrot, sneaking into the guestroom to go potty. We all miss you. Me the most, of course.

Thank you for your sweetness, your love, your enthusiasm. You never questioned whether you belonged here or whether you deserved all the best. You just took it and ran – literally. Life – you had it all on lock.

Love, Mom

August 4, 2019
You were so full of life this world could not hold you.

August 5, 2019
Have you ever noticed how you can only see the true beauty of a gem when looking at it at an angle, not straight on? Straight on, you can see the color and shape, but the true sparkling beauty is in its reflection of light.

I think that's how it is with pain and loss. Looking straight at it, you see the flat fact of it. Death. Gone. Final (at least in this lifetime).

Move away a little and glance back there. See that? That glint, that sparkle, especially as the light passes through it? That's the true essence of what we've lost. It's still there if you look at it from the right angle.

Bryn, the essence of you, your sparkle and glint will never leave my heart. Thank you.

August 13, 2019

Lucky had an appointment for a rabies booster and nail trim. I was dreading it because of his reaction to the rabies vaccine three years prior.

However, all went well. Our favorite tech checked him in, and she gave him his weight's worth in treats. They took him back and performed the necessary deeds.

All good, I thought. I heard the vet but didn't think we needed to talk. We ran into each other in the hallway.

"How are you?" he asked.

"Okay," I answered.

Then he told me he wanted another Benadryl for Lucky that evening.

"Thanks," I said.

I made it past the desk, out the door, and into the car. Then the tears started.

It would have been so much easier if everyone had been clumsy and mean. Anger and unforgiveness are easy to hold on to; gripping onto them keeps the hurt and tears from pouring out.

But just one person asking to your face, "How are you?" Why is that too much? Over the phone or by email is no big deal. "I'm fine. I'm better. I'm moving along." It's the look. You can see it in their eyes.

Anyway, still hurts Bryn.

August 23, 2019

Did I love you enough in the short time we had?

August 29, 2019

On Earth for but a moment; in our hearts for eternity. You touched this earth lightly and quickly, and like a shot, you were off to the heavens.

September 7, 2019

Bryn, you were too good for this earth. I don't mean good as in sinless. I mean good, as in all the good things rolled into one. Good as in bringing warmth and love to every participant in your life. Life's weight, pain, and darkness could not abide your light, love, and joy. You are in the Light of His presence now. Bask in its rays, in the goodness of His perfection.

The Work of Healing

the work of healing
means remembering with love
while moving forward

Together, we've journeyed through the six stages of grief – on paper, that is. However, healing often involves some physical labor to get our bodies and spirits back on track. Just like we may need physical therapy after an injury or surgery, our minds and hearts can benefit from an emotion "workout".

Following is a list of 30 activities you can do in any order. Completing one per day is probably too much, as some of the practices take mulling over and some require more than a paper and pen. How ever it works for you is the right way. One a day or one a week, working through them as the mood and timing strikes you, or starting with the small things until you've created something large are all fine ideas.

I suggest these exercises so that you can further explore your feelings and stretch your healing muscles. Not all the activities will appeal to everyone, and some won't apply to you. I have done many, but not all of them in my healing journey.

If you're resistant to a particular theme, such as anything involving forgiveness or sharing with others, then consider why that may be. Could you be stuck in a particular phase of grieving? Is it a sign that speaking with a mental health professional might help you move along in your journey? Maybe you simply don't enjoy writing things down. If drawing pictures or talking to others or sharing on social media are more comfortable for you, then go that route. Some of the ideas may catch on and you might choose to keep that daily or weekly practice for as long as it suits you. This is your show, your grief, and your healing. Do it your way.

If you are inclined toward journaling or recording your thoughts and feelings, here are a couple of simple ideas to get you started. Feel free to handwrite in a notebook, type into your computer, or jot thoughts on a calendar. First, try writing your feelings each morning and night – as much or as little as you want. It can be as little as "crappy" or "tired" or as many pages as you want to go. Record your energy and emotional highs and lows of each day. When were you at your best? When did you feel your worst? What were you doing? Who were you with? It can be that simple. There's no need to analyze what you've written unless you feel like it or start noticing disturbing patterns.

Here are 30 things you can do to build up your healing muscles while also memorializing your pet and honoring their importance in your life.

1. Write a eulogy for your pet. What would you and others say about them at a memorial? Would there be laughter? How do you want others to remember your pet? Share this with people who loved your pet, if you feel comfortable doing so. They will appreciate it.

2. Write your pet's epitaph. What would you put on their permanent grave marker? Consider creating or purchasing a permanent

marker for your pet – inside or outside, depending on your living situation.

3. Go through each item belonging to or pertaining to your lost pet: beds, blankets, toys, food containers, medicines, etc. Decide if you want to save them as a keepsake, keep them for another pet, give them to charity, or discard them. Responsibly discard of all prescription medicines. When you're ready, wash all the items and store them properly as keepsakes or for a future pet, or give them away.

4. What are your favorite memories of your pet? Write about them or find photos and put them in an album (digital or paper copy). You can record silly times, trips you took, when they comforted you, or how you found each other, for starters.

5. What would your pet's life motto be? Why? Examples might be "Leave no shoe unchewed", or "To love me is to smell me", or "Barking is how I say, 'I love you'".

6. Write about a time you were mad at or frustrated with your pet. What did you do? How did you feel after you calmed down? How did the pet react during and after the event? If your pet were here now, what would you say to them? Tell them now. They forgive you, and they know you love and miss them.

7. What do you think your pet would say to you today? How would that make you feel? How would you respond?

8. Write any type of poem of any length about your pet or your feelings. Some examples of poetry forms are: rhyming, couplet, limerick, sonnet, and free verse. You can find more forms and

examples of each online. Don't be your own critic. The poem doesn't have to be good; it just has to be from you and about your pet or your feelings.

9. Write a haiku about your pet. There are several types of haiku, but the most common is the 5-7-5 form. It consists of three lines – the first line containing five syllables, the second line comprising seven syllables, and the third line containing five syllables. Typically, haiku does not rhyme, should contain a minimum of punctuation, and frequently the topic is nature or a moment in time. For ideas, there are several examples in this book, as well as online.

10. Write the story of your pet's life. If you know their parental history, start with that. If the pet came to you as an adult, start with the birth of your relationship. What brought you together? Was it a happy accident or planned? Who needed whom the most? Write about the fun times and the pain-in-the-butt times. Think about their favorite places, trips, and foods. Write all the way to the end. This will probably take longer than one sitting, and that's okay. You'll probably think of more things to add.

11. Write the story of your pet's death. Write about the illness, the decline, or the accident. What was their reaction, your reaction, and others' reactions? Was it a "good" death (comfortable, pain-free, secure)? Or was it a hard death (traumatic, sudden, painful for the animal)? Who helped make it better? Who do you feel made it worse? What did you choose to do with your pet's remains? How do you feel about that choice now? How would you handle the passing differently if you had to do it over again? What would you do exactly the same?

12. Do you have any feelings of personal responsibility or guilt around your pet's death? Write about the specifics and how you feel about it. Was there something that could have been avoided, or was the progression of events inevitable? Write a letter of forgiveness to yourself from your pet now that they are in a comfortable, pain-free existence. If talking feels easier to you than writing, tell a supportive, trusted person about your feelings. If possible and appropriate, repair the circumstances that led to the loss. For example, fix a broken fence or invest in pet insurance for your remaining pets.

13. Write a song for or about your pet. If you can set it to music (original or not) all the better. If creating a song isn't your cup of tea, think about what your pet's theme song might be.

14. Write a fictional or true story starring your pet. It can be as long or as short as you'd like. This can be funny, sad, inspiring, or whatever feelings you'd like to convey.

15. Think about the silliest thing you ever bought for your pet and the best thing you ever bought for them. Would you buy those things again?

16. Who was your pet's favorite person, after you? Have you reminisced with them or shared something belonging to the pet with them, even a photograph?

17. Make a collage, or draw or paint a picture of your pet and his/her life.

18. Create a memory box or scrapbook page of your pet's life (as many pages as you need).

19. Write a thank-you letter or note to all friends and family who cared for and helped with your pet during their good times and bad times.

20. Write a thank-you letter to your pet for being part of your life and bringing you joy.

21. Write a thank-you letter to your pet's healthcare providers. If that seems disingenuous, write a letter of grievance, then put it away or give it to a trustworthy friend to hold on to for you until you are ready to let go of the grievance. When you are ready, you may want to destroy the letter, or you may want to save with your keepsakes as a reminder of your strength in healing.

22. Write a letter to other pet owners telling them what you've learned and what might help them during pet ownership and loss. You can share this on social media or find an online pet site, pet magazine, or personal essay publication where you could submit the piece for possible publication.

23. Write a letter to a non-animal person, explaining your feelings and forgiving (if necessary) their lack of understanding and/or empathy. This is for you, not to be sent out, although this could possibly be an open letter, addressed to Anonymous, that might be published somewhere.

24. Write a letter of comfort to yourself. Tell yourself how proud you are of how you've handled this loss and how brave you are to have loved one that you knew would likely leave you first. Remind yourself that you've done an honorable thing loving this animal, risking your heart, and providing them with a good life, and good death, if applicable.

25. Make a list of ways in which you could honor your pet through service, such as free pet sitting, volunteering at a shelter, fostering animals, walking the pets of the ill, disabled, or aged, taking the disabled and their pets to appointments, picking up pet meds for the homebound, shopping for pet supplies for others, taking pets to the groomer/vet, or taking pets to dog parks. Consider donating or becoming involved with animal charities specific to your species/breed or other animal welfare charities, especially organizations in your local area.

26. Consider the five stages of grief and how you've experienced them so far. How do you see your grief experience evolving in the future? What do you dread? How might you mitigate future pain? What are you looking forward to?

27. If you were to get a new pet, what are some names you'd consider giving it? Keep a running list, even if you are not currently seeking a new pet. Of course, you may want the name to fit the personality, so the final naming will have to wait, but doing this can help open your heart to a new love.

28. What are some different breeds or species you might bring into your home in the future? Sometimes, switching from dog to cat or vice versa will help decrease the risk of unrealistic expectations of the new pet, as well as teach us new ways to relate to an animal. When you get an idea, investigate it. Learn what you can about that type of animal – for future reference. You can search on the internet, join online groups, and talk to others who are more knowledgeable about that type of pet. Online forums have tons of people who don't actually own that type of pet but love them and are animal advocates. You can learn a lot from them.

29. What do you miss the most about your pet? What don't you miss (no guilt feelings allowed!)? It can be as simple as "no longer vacuuming hairs out of the couch" to "not having to spend so much money on medications." Acknowledging that some burdens have lightened does not mean we wouldn't take our pets back in a second if we could. This is just a way of allowing your mind to lean in a more positive direction and hopefully provide emotional balance and a realistic view of what taking on a new pet will likely entail.

30. What can you do now – because you have more time, money, and/or freedom – that you couldn't do or were holding off on doing while your pet was living with you? Think about experiencing some of those things now. Examples include taking a long trip that isn't pet-friendly or inviting non-animal people over for a visit. Now's the time to think about large-scale home improvements that would have been difficult with a full-time pet, such as rebuilding your entire fence, remodeling the kitchen, re-carpeting the house, or installing new external doors or windows.

I hope these have provided you with some helpful ideas. If you have other practices and rituals that have been healing for you, I'd love to hear about them!

Conclusion

Things Bryn taught me:
Run while you can.
Don't wait for permission.
You can get away with a lot if you live passionately, are cute,
and never hold back on love or enthusiasm.
Love can really hurt, but it's worth the risk.
You don't have to be beautiful to be adored.
You are worthy of love by existing.
Be yourself.
When someone is singing to you, don't just listen, dance.
You can feel happiness and still be grieving.

You and I have been down a hard road. We didn't meet until we were at one of the hardest places on our life journey — the loss of a beloved pet. For most of us pet lovers, this will be a situation we'll find ourselves in multiple times. Sometimes the loss will be harder than other times. There are so many factors that impact this, we don't have to analyze it much. Why does the death of certain pets hit us harder than others? We may know the answer, or it may make no sense. Regardless, we know we love, and we know we'll love again. For now, it's hard, and we must properly mourn and free our beloved to run or fly in a new place.

I hope and pray this little book has helped you. If it has provided a lamp to help guide you through the dark woods of grief, it's fulfilled its purpose. I hope it's given you a place and a practice to record your experiences and feelings through words and visual or musical arts. I also hope it's given you space to forgive and to remember sweet, good times.

As I mentioned in the beginning, Elizabeth Kubler-Ross' grief stages framework is not endorsed by all grief counselors. Instead of the sixth stage of finding meaning, some professionals have added a sixth stage called "renewal". Others have eschewed the Kubler-Ross framework entirely. However, I, and many others, have found Kubler-Ross' and Kessler's stages clear and helpful. Grief is a journey with many possible paths. I hope this book helps you find the one that's best for you.

Please share if you know anyone who might be able to use bits from this book. They may want their own copy; that's up to you if you want to pass it along.

If you found comfort in these words, I'd love to hear from you. I also would enjoy learning about your pets. You can send your stories and photos to tiffany@tiffanydickinson.com. If you're open to them being made public, let me know. Otherwise, you and I can simply share.

Feel free to send me additional pet grief support resources that you've found helpful. I can add them to my list of resources on my website.

If you'd like to get my latest release news and author updates in your email, please sign up for my newsletter at www.tiffanydickinson.com. I send emails twice monthly. A bonus, if you follow me, is more pictures of the rascals living with us: Lola, Misha, and Bridget.

Lastly, it would be lovely if you'd leave a review on your favorite site so that others can find this book and get the support and encouragement they need.

Thank you for reading and Happy Healing.

References

Clark, Samantha. www.societyforpsychotherapy.org *Traumatic Pet Loss*. Accessed May 21, 2023. https://societyforpsychotherapy.org/traumatic-pet-loss/

Handler, Jessica. *Braving the Fire: A Guide to Writing About Grief and Loss*. New York. St. Martin's Griffin. 2013.

Kessler, David. *Finding Meaning*. New York. Simon & Schuster. 2019.

Kurz, Gary. *Cold Noses at the Pearly Gates*. New York. Citadel Press Books. 2008.

Rogers, Kristen. www.cnn.com. Updated May 15, 2023. https://www.cnn.com/2021/09/12/health/five-stages-of-grief-kubler-ross-meaning-wellness/

www.humanesociety.org. https://humanepro.org/page/pets-by-the-numbers. Updated 2023.

Online Resources

www.compassionspeaks.com From the website home page: "Compassionate animal communication. Bridging the Gap of Understanding between people and their pets."

www.wendyvandepoll.com From the website home page: "Animal Advocate". Books and counseling resources available for grieving pet lovers.

www.rainbowsbridge.com From the website home page: "Rainbows Bridge is a virtual memorial home and grief support community for your departed fur baby. Whether furry, feathered or scaled, all are welcome."

Acknowledgements

First, I'd like to thank my husband Paul for his tireless support, frequent hugs when writing this book brought me to tears, and his prodding me to continue on. Sometimes nagging is a good thing.

Bottomless thanks to my beta readers Marsha Dickinson and Kathy Perrin, who provided incalculable help on this manuscript, telling me what worked and what did not. I appreciate their insights, especially as they were reminded of the losses of their own dear pets.

Many thanks to Allison Behrens, editor extraordinaire, who, among many other things, caught the repeats in the manuscript and the extra syllables in several haiku. What is a writer without an editor?

Thank you to my mother, Lorisa Gardiner, who told me all the poetry needed to be in the book. As a poetry lover, she was sure other poetry lovers would seek it out. I think she's right.

To all who supported me and gave me love during and after losing Bryn. Family and friends, you kept me off the ledge by listening to me and empathizing.

Last, but not least, I also appreciate the many animal lovers I've encountered as I've worked on this book who told me how important this book is and that it is needed.

Thank you!

About the Author

I write, rubbing the nubs on the pen you chewed while under the bed.
I press gently, feeling where your teeth sought pleasure.
Hoping the ink will last forever.

Tiffany Dickinson is the author of two middle grade novels and one nonfiction book. She lives in southwest Washington in the United States with two nutsy black pugs and a part-feral black cat. They allow her husband to live there too, especially since he sneaks them the best treats. When not writing, Tiffany is walking with the pugs around Lake Sacajawea, trying to get to the beach, or zooming along Interstate 5 to get grandbaby snuggles.

Connect with Tiffany on her website: www.tiffanydickinson.com. For updates on the pet-loving writer life and upcoming events and book releases, sign up for her email newsletter. Find her on Facebook and Instagram, as well. Share your animal pictures and stories! Follow her on Facebook for more pictures and anecdotes about Bridget and Misha (and sometimes Lola when she's speaking to them).

By Tiffany Dickinson

Kaleidoscope – middle grade historical fiction,
set in Portland, Oregon in 1980
A Mink's Tale – middle grade animal fantasy,
set in the Western United States
Healing from Pet Loss:
The Journey from Loving to Losing to Living Again
Find them everywhere books are sold!

Made in the USA
Monee, IL
17 October 2023